D0410709

THE GREAT
BRITISH
BREAKFAST

Also by Jan Read and Maite Manjón

Jan Read
THE WINES OF SPAIN AND PORTUGAL (Faber)
THE MOORS IN SPAIN AND PORTUGAL (Faber)
WAR IN THE PENINSULA (Faber)
LORD COCHRANE (Plata Press)
GUIDE TO THE WINES OF SPAIN AND PORTUGAL (Pitman)
THE CATALANS (Faber)
THE NEW CONQUISTADORES Evans)

with Antonio Mingote
HISTORY FOR BEGINNERS (Nelson)

Maite Manjón
THE HOME BOOK OF PORTUGUESE COOKERY (Faber)

with Catherine O'Brien
SPANISH COOKING AT HOME AND ON HOLIDAY (Pan)

Jan Read and Maite Manjón
PARADORES OF SPAIN (Macmillan)
FLAVOURS OF SPAIN (Cassell)
VISITORS' SCOTLAND (Macmillan)

THE GREAT BRITISH BREAKFAST

Jan Read and
Maite Manjón

MICHAEL JOSEPH · LONDON

First published in Great Britain by
Michael Joseph Ltd
44 Bedford Square, London WC1
1981

© 1981 by Jan Read and Maite Manjón

Published in association with
Limelight Ltd, and Frank Cooper.
Frank Cooper is a trademark
of CPC (United Kingdom) Ltd

All Rights Reserved. No part of this
publication may be reproduced, stored in a
retrieval system, or transmitted in any form
or by any means, electronic, mechanical,
photocopying, recording or otherwise,
without the prior permission of the
Copyright owner

ISBN 0 7181 2004 3

Composition by Alacrity Phototypesetters,
Banwell Castle, Avon. Printed in Great
Britain by Hollen Street Press, Slough
and bound by Hunter and Foulis,
Edinburgh

Contents

Illustrations

Colour Illustrations

Acknowledgements

WE ARE GRATEFUL to Alexander Maclehose & Co for permission to reproduce the recipes from F. Marian McNeill's *The Book of Breakfasts*; to B. T. Batsford & Co for the short extracts from Thomas Burke's *Travel in England*; to the Rank Organisation for the quotation from Dylan Thomas's *Me and My Bike*; to Paul Jennings and Eyre and Spottiswoode Ltd for the sketch from *The Railway Lover's Companion*; To William Heinemann Ltd for the quotation from W. Somerset Maugham's *Three Fat Women of Antibes*; to O. S. Nock and Ian Allen Ltd for the dialogue from *The Railway Races to the North*; and to Ralph Pomeroy and the Paddington Press for permission to reproduce a passage from *First Things First*. Our special thanks are due to Frank Cooper's Oxford Marmalade Ltd for allowing us access to their records and for help over the chapter on marmalade.

The illustrations have come from a variety of sources and we should particularly like to thank Mr Raymond O'Shea and Baynton Williams Ltd, Mrs Anne O'Shea, Mr Julian Armytage and Armytage Clark Ltd, British Transport Hotels and Travellers-Fare, the National Railway Museum, The National Maritime Museum, Cunard-White Star Ltd and the Camden and Westminster Public Libraries.

Foreword

'If you would eat well in England, you must eat breakfast three times a day.'

W. Somerset Maugham

IN A HAND-TO-MOUTH WORLD where breakfast has often shrunk to no more than a cup of instant coffee, supplemented at best by a glass of fruit juice and a little cereal, books on breakfasting are out of fashion. One can look for them in vain in bookshops full to overflowing with volumes on Chinese and Polynesian food, compilations of favourite dishes by film stars or thriller writers, quick-freeze books, pressure-cooker books, cook-it-the-day-before books, coffee-table tomes by famous chefs, or pocket-size companions for calorie counters.

This was not always so. During the hey-day of the traditional British breakfast, perhaps served in its most elaborate form in country houses during the nineteenth century, numerous books on the subject were published. Among them were such gems as *Breakfasts, Luncheons, and Ball Suppers* by Major L... (also author of the *Pytchley Book of Refined Cookery and Bills of Fare*); *Breakfasts and Savoury Dishes* by R. O. C. (of the National Training School for Cooking); and *Fifty Breakfasts* by 'Wyvern' (Colonel Kenney-Herbert) — retired military gentlemen were seemingly the foremost exponents of the genre. And as late as 1932, F. Marian McNeill published *The Book of Breakfasts*, written with all her usual scholarship and feeling for the traditions of her native Scotland.

Of these, more later — but *is* the traditional British breakfast anything more than a nostalgic memory? It would seem not. Even in 1887, Major L..., foreshadowing the shape of things to come, could write:

He thinks the reader will agree with him that, as a rule, in England, breakfast is not sufficiently considered; that a good breakfast is the exception and not the rule, and that one sees either an *embarras de*

11

richesses in the shape of pounds of mutton chops, beefsteaks, kidneys, and the everlasting (although excellent, if the eggs are fresh and the bacon good) eggs and bacon; or, on the other hand, barely sufficient of the overnight's repast ...

But ask any travel agent what the foreign visitor considers to be the requisites of an enjoyable holiday in Britain. High on the list comes the provision of a hotel serving substantial British breakfasts. It would appear that, once across the Channel, the visiting Frenchman or Spaniard turns his back on coffee and *croissants* and that he not only expects, but positively demands, bacon and eggs, Cumberland sausage, kippers and Oxford marmalade.

Recent figures issued by British Rail, leading exponents of the Great British Breakfast, as it is described on their menus, reinforce the point. Of two-and-a-quarter million meals served in railway restaurant cars in 1978, 915,500 were breakfasts, 646,900 lunches and 440,400 dinners. Most of them were, of course, consumed by natives — breakfast is especially popular on early trains catering for businessmen — so that it would seem that the Briton is still keen enough on his breakfast, provided it is put in front of him and he has leisure to do justice to it. When kippers disappeared from the menu of the late-lamented Brighton Belle, it became a matter of national concern after Sir Laurence Olivier wrote a letter of complaint to *The Times*.

According to Webster's *Third New International Dictionary* the probable derivation of the word 'breakfast' is from the Middle English *brekfast*, in turn derived from *breken*, to 'break', and 'fast'. The overnight interval without nourishment is the longest in the twenty-four hours, so that it would seem logical to break one's fast by eating enough of the right sort of food to supply energy for the morning's activities. Clearly, a cup of coffee contains next to no sustenance, while medical evidence shows that the cereal which often accompanies it provides a quick, but fairly rapidly diminishing, increase in the blood sugar supplying the energy for bodily needs. This is a controversial subject which we shall be considering in Chapter IX, but the consensus of medical opinion is that a high-protein meal produces slow and lasting increases in blood sugar and is the best preparation for the day's work ahead. Tradition, as so often, makes good sense; if you like a good breakfast, enjoy it without qualms!

A study of old books and manuscripts reveals that there is virtually no dish which the British, at one time or another, have not eaten and enjoyed

An advertisement for Colonel Kenney Herbert's ('Wyvern's') cookery school, c. 1890

THE COMMON-SENSE

Cookery Association.

Managing Director:

COLONEL KENNEY HERBERT.

The objects of this Association are :—

(1) To provide Lectures in which the rules of good, refined, and economical Cookery will be explained and practically demonstrated.

(2) To afford opportunities of systematic instruction at moderate cost to Students, Cooks, and others, who are desirous of attaining to efficiency and to qualify for good situations.

(3) To establish a Registry for Cooks whose antecedents have been ascertained and qualifications tested, and who can, accordingly, be with confidence recommended.

The Registry has been opened at 13, Sloane Street, and the Lectures are delivered on Mondays at the Queen's Gate Hall. Particulars obtainable at GASTRELL'S LIBRARY, 15, Sussex Place, South Kensington.

for breakfast. At one end of the scale was the eccentric Mrs Jeffreys, sister of the restless eighteenth-century political agitator John Wilkes, who broke her fast frugally on chocolate and dry toast — only to dine off slices of fat cut off a huge joint, washed down with old Madeira and swallowed alternately with lumps of chalk, supposedly to neutralise the acids of the meat. She lived to a ripe old age and enjoyed perfect health. At the opposite extreme were the vast breakfasts eaten at country houses in the eighteenth and nineteenth centuries, which might, for example, progress from kedgeree to devilled pheasant, broiled ham, mutton chops and eggs, with a selection of cold meats on the side and further accompanied by an assortment of breads, toast, muffins, preserves and fruit.

We have included in this book recipes for most of the breakfast dishes popular today. Others, taken from contemporary books, are somewhat ambitious for streamlined meals, but if eaten singly and not by the half dozen, might enliven the breakfast table — at least at the weekend, when there is more time for cooking, and breakfast often merges into lunch. Rather than simply naming some of those dishes so dear to our forebears — such as Frumenty, Hashed Mutton and Pickled Walnuts, Devilled Kidneys, Sally Lunns and the rest — it seemed of interest to give working instructions for making them. We, at any rate, have enjoyed re-creating and sampling them, as we hope you will too, if not at breakfast, perhaps at suppertime.

There is an art even in the cooking of simple things, such as porridge, boiled eggs, toast and kippers (how many Sassenachs plunge them into boiling water?), and proper and improper methods of preparing them. And we have tried to be explicit and to the point, like Dr William Kitchener, who wrote in his *Cook's Oracle* of 1817 that he had 'eaten each receipt before he set it down in his book' and that he 'found [precision] indispensable from the impossibility of guessing the quantities intended by such obscure expressions as have usually been employed for this purpose in former works; for instance, a bit of this, a handful of that, a pinch of t'other — do 'em over with an egg, and shake of pepper, a squeeze of lemon or a dash of vinegar, are the constant phrases; season it to your palate (meaning the cook's) if she has any....'

CHAPTER I

A Little History

'Tell me what you eat and I will tell you what you are.'
Brillat Savarin

THE BRITISH have so long been known for their substantial breakfasts that one is tempted to believe that it is an institution whose origins are lost in the mists of history. This is not so; and the most cursory study soon reveals that there have been continuous changes in the style and manner of eating. The very abundance of the breakfasts consumed by the well-to-do during the eighteenth and nineteenth centuries points to a regimen very different from today's.

In Saxon and mediaeval times only two main meals were eaten: one at about eight or nine in the morning and the other around four in the afternoon. As late as 1597, an early traveller in the Scottish Highlands, Monipennie, commented that the people 'made only two meals in the day — the *little* meal about noon, and the *great* meal towards evening.' With variations in the timing, and sometimes supplemented by a late supper, this two-meal pattern persisted in the British Isles until the beginnings of the nineteenth century, when breakfast was in the main a masculine meal. Among the upper classes at that time the husband would eat early and substantially, while his wife would breakfast lightly at about 10 a.m., perhaps on cakes and tea or chocolate. Even in 1887, Major L . . ., writing about meals appropriate to country houses, describes lunch as 'the ladies' meal' and counsels that it should be light — though ideas on quantity have changed. For such a delicate repast he considers 'an entrée, a roast, and a pudding quite sufficient.'

In more mundane circles, eating patterns had begun to change with the onset of the Industrial Revolution. For centuries England had been a predominantly rural society with work confined to the daylight hours. In the new mills and factories, labourers might work for fourteen hours with brief intervals during the day for breakfast and dinner; and the old four o'clock family dinner no longer met the needs of the new urban professional classes. With dinner timed later to await the return of the bread-winner and midday lunch becoming habitual, it was inevitable that breakfast should diminish in importance.

What was actually eaten at breakfast in early times depended, of course, on circumstances and occupation. We are told that the Saxons breakfasted on cold pork, dark bread and ale, and that in the Middle Ages the rich ate boiled beef, mutton and pickled herring, washed down with ale and wine. One traditional breakfast dish in mediaeval times was frumenty, which was to the English what porridge is to the Scots. It was made by steeping new wheat in warm water, hulling and drying the grain and then boiling it in milk, and was sweetened and spiced before serving.

'*Breakfast with* The Times' (*Cassell's* Family Magazine, *1878*)

In Tudor times, farmers and farm labourers ate heartily of bread, butter, cheese and bacon, while Good Queen Bess and her maids, according to a Dr Doran, 'both dined and breakfasted upon very solid principles and materials. Beef and beer were consumed at breakfast — "a repast for a ploughman!" it may be said . . . .'

Tea and coffee, which revolutionised breakfast habits, were not commonly available in England until the latter part of the seventeenth century, and, as Charles Cooper reports in *The English Table in History and Literature*, 'What Gloriana was most particular about was the quality of her malt liquor, and [during her royal progresses] particular care was enjoined to ascertain how far the beer of the country would suit the Queen's taste, as otherwise it would be necessary to forward supplies from London.'

The Scots, of course, have from time immemorial breakfasted on brochan — or, in its anglicised form, porridge — of which M. Martin, Gent., wrote in his *Description of the Western Isles* in 1703 that 'oatmeal boiled with water, with some [barley] bread, is the constant food of both sexes in this and other islands during winter and spring, yet they go under many fatigues by sea and land, and are very healthful.'

Especially in the Highlands, the diet of country people was frugal and barely reached subsistence levels during the hard winters. Even as late as 1732 in more affluent St Andrews the daily ration of the foundationers who lived in college was 'a scone and a third, a pint of meagre ale, some salt or fresh beef, veal, or mutton (or, alternatively, fowl or fish) at dinner, and at supper three eggs "or what is equivalent of wheat bread".' The ternar, who lived out of college, made do on even shorter commons, his main sustenance being the oatmeal brought from his father's farm in Fife or Forfar. In February the University still observes a holiday on Meal Monday, when it was the custom for students to return home and replenish the stock.

Fruit was very little eaten in Britain at breakfast or at other meals during the early period, except by the rich; and, indeed, street fruiterers in the sixteenth century were forbidden to sell plums and apples, since it was considered that servants and apprentices might steal from their employers to buy them. The scarcity of vegetables was in fact probably responsible for the prevalence of leprosy and similar diseases until late Stuart times. Dr Felix Oswald, quoted by Charles Cooper, has even suggested that the supposed efficacy of the 'royal touch' resulted not so much from any gift bestowed upon the king from on high, but from the wild herbs and berries consumed by the afflicted on the high road to London.

As regards the more substantial meat dishes eaten by the better-to-do at breakfast, until the seventeenth century, roast meats were notable for their absence. This resulted from the lack of table implements other than spoons with which to eat them, so that even at dinner the principal dishes were soups, potages, stews and hashes. Entire joints were never served except in royal and noble households, where the carver, often a knight or gentleman of lineage, would first cut a slice of meat with a large, sharp-pointed knife, then further cut it into four strips for the greater part of its length. The meat was held at the uncut end, while the diner gnawed at the appendages.

Forks, which made possible the carving of meat on the plate, were introduced to England from Italy by Thomas Coryate, author of the famous *Coryate's Crudities*, after a tour of the Continent in 1601; and the use of round-ended knives at table is traditionally credited to Cardinal Richelieu. It seems that he was so disgusted to see his guests 'washing their fingers in the sauce' and using their pointed knives as toothpicks that he summarily forbade their use at table; and in 1669 an edict was promulgated in France prohibiting '*toutes personnes de quelque qualité qu'elles soient de porter couteaux pointus aux couteliers, et autres marchands d'en fabriquer, vendre et débiter.*'

G. M. Trevelyan notes that in the middle of the seventeenth century many upper and middle-class families breakfasted on no more than a 'morning draft' of ale with a little bread and butter; but with the table implements now available, the way was henceforth open to the splendid side tables, with their array of cold hams, tongues and rounds of beef, so necessary to a well-conducted breakfast in the eighteenth and nineteenth centuries.

By now the introduction of tea and coffee (see Chapter IX) in place of beer, ale and wine had further transformed the breakfast table, so that by 1729 a Highlander from the far extreme of the kingdom, Mackintosh of Borlum, gave rise to the plaintive lament:

When I came to a friend's house of a morning I used to be asked if I had had my morning draft yet. I am now asked if I have had my tea. And in lieu of the big quaigh with strong ale and toast, and after a dram of good wholesome Scots spirits, there is now the tea-kettle put to the fire, the tea-table and silver and china equipage brought in, and marmalade and cream.

'The Fat Kitchin and the Lean Kitchin' (eighteenth-century print)

The diet of labourers and the poor during the halcyon days of the Great British Breakfast bore little relation to that of their more fortunate compatriots, and Ralph Pomeroy in *First Things First* has reproduced a blow-by-blow account of what was eaten in a Bishopsgate workhouse during the early years of the eighteenth century.

> They have Breakfasts, dinners and suppers every day in the week. For each meal 4oz. of bread, 1½oz. cheese, 1oz butter, 1 pint beer. Breakfast four days, bread and cheese or butter and beer. Monday a pint of pease pottage, with Bread and Beer. Tuesdays a Plumb Pudding Pye, 9 oz., and beer. Wednesdays a pint of frumity [frumenty, see p16]. On Friday a pint of barley broth and bread. On Saturdays a plain flower suet Dumpling with beer...

Even this seems more ample than the food an industrious labourer could afford a century later, which Sir William Eden, writing in 1797, described as follows: Sunday, bread and cheese; Monday, broth; Tuesday, bread and cheese; Wednesday, same as Monday; Thursday, same as Tuesday; Friday, same as Monday; Saturday, bread and cheese.

But our purpose is to describe the pristine glories of the British breakfast table, and in the soldierly words of Major L..., 'the object not being to make a book, but to give really useful information, we proceed at once to the task.'

EGGS

There are dozens of ways of cooking eggs; but at breakfast they are usually served boiled, fried, poached, scrambled, baked in the oven or as an omelette.

Boiled Eggs
Boiling an egg is probably the first tentative step in cooking that most of us take. It is often regarded as easy, but in fact demands great nicety of timing. To begin with, most people like a boiled egg with the white just set and the yolk runny, but others prefer it soft boiled and runny, or even hard. Again, the cooking time depends upon size and freshness. There are three grades of eggs: those fresh from the nest (or up to three days old); 'new-laid' eggs, which may be up to two or three weeks old; and, as Philip Harben once said, 'curate's eggs'.

20

The procedure with a normal 'new-laid' egg of medium size (2½ oz.) is first to check that it is not cracked — otherwise it may exude festoons of half-set white — and to lower it gently with a spoon into a pan of boiling water. The cooking time for a 'medium boiled' egg is four minutes; large eggs or average-sized fresh eggs require a minute more, and soft boiled a minute less. Hard-boiled eggs may safely be left for ten minutes.

In her now classical *Modern Cookery* of 1845, Eliza Acton recommends the following alternative method:

'First, put some boiling water into a large basin — a slop-basin for example — and let it remain for a few seconds, then turn it out, lay in the egg (or eggs), and roll it over to take the chill off the shell, that it may not crack from the sudden application of heat; and pour in — and upon the egg — *quite boiling* water from a kettle, until it is completely immersed; put a plate over it instantly, and let it remain, upon the table, for twelve minutes, when it will be found perfectly and beautifully cooked, entirely free from all flavour and appearance of *rawness*, and yet so lightly and delicately dressed as to suit even persons who cannot take eggs at all when boiled in the usual way. It should be turned when something more than half done, but the plate should be replaced as soon as possible. Two eggs will require scarcely more time than one; but some additional minutes must be allowed for any number beyond that.'

Fried Eggs

The traditional English way of frying eggs is to do so in fat (and there is nothing better than the bacon fat which drops from the grill) that is *fairly* hot, but not smoking. The white will then set, but remain soft. To avoid accidents with broken yolks or bad eggs, a sensible precaution is to break the egg into a cup and then slide it into the hot fat in the frying pan. Fried eggs should be basted, by tilting the pan and ladling a little of the hot fat over the yolk.

An alternative method, popular in Spain, is to use olive oil or cooking oil and, without burning it, to heat it more strongly in the frying pan until a haze arises. When fried in this way, the whites of the eggs are crisp and crinkly — it is very much a matter of personal taste.

Poached Eggs

To poach eggs in the old-fashioned way, boil some lightly-salted water in a small saucepan or deep frying pan. Break the eggs individually into a cup, taking care to keep the yolk whole. Remove the pan to the side of the fire, slide in the egg, gently fold the white over the yolk with a table-spoon, then simmer until the white is set. Remove carefully with a slotted spoon and trim the edges.

Nowadays most people find it easier to use a special pan with removable aluminium 'shapes'. Lightly grease the 'shapes' with butter and slide the eggs into them from a cup. Meanwhile bring some water to the boil in the pan, put the 'shapes' in position and cover with the lid. Simmer until the whites have set up to the edges of the yolk, which should be soft and just 'veiled'. Turn out carefully on to hot-buttered toast and dust with a little pepper and salt.

Scrambled Eggs

Break the eggs into a bowl, season with salt and pepper, add a little cream if you wish, and beat lightly — but not as thoroughly as for an omelette. The conventional wisdom is now to melt a knob of butter in a saucepan, rotating it to coat the bottom and sides, and then to add the egg mixture. In fact, it is simpler and does not affect the final result, to add the butter with the egg mixture; and the most important thing in making scrambled eggs is to cook them over a very low fire, stirring continuously with a wooden spoon. When lumps begin forming at the bottom of the pan, it is a sign that cooking is on the way to completion. Continue stirring, but do not allow the mixture to become dry or stringy and pour it out while it is still on the fluid side, as it will firm up a little and, though thick, should be smooth and creamy when served.

Scrambled eggs are usually served on fried bread or buttered or hot-buttered toast, and savoury versions may be made by stirring into the egg mixture a variety of minced, chopped or flaked ingredients, such as previously cooked ham, chicken livers or Finnan haddock. Blanched tomatoes and grated cheese also go well with them.

Eggs in the Oven

This is a good way of cooking eggs, if you have an Aga or similar type of stove.

Lightly butter some individual fireproof dishes. Carefully break an egg into each and season with salt and pepper. Place the dishes in a hot oven and bake for about five minutes or until the whites are set. As a variant, place a couple of rashers of bacon in the bottom of the dish, cook in the oven for five minutes, so releasing a little fat, then break in the egg and bake for another five minutes.

Omelettes

For some reason British cooks often make heavy weather of making omelettes, and they are frequently served too dry; but there is no difficulty about making a good plain omelette.

Break a couple of eggs into a bowl, season with salt and pepper, add a teaspoon of water per egg and beat well with a fork. Do not over-beat or the omelette will end up with more of the consistency of a soufflé, instead of soft and creamy in the middle. Meanwhile, melt a knob of butter in a heavy frying pan and heat until it is on the point of smoking, but without allowing it to brown. Pour in the egg mixture and let the bottom surface set, then vigorously shake the pan, or if you find it easier, keep pulling back the edges with a fork and tilting the pan, so that the uncooked mixture comes into contact with the hot metal. Before the mixture at the centre is entirely set, slide a palette knife under the omelette, fold it and slide on to a pre-heated plate.

Savoury omelettes are made by stirring into the egg mixture herbs or any of the ingredients suggested for scrambled eggs.

CHAPTER II

Country-House Breakfasts

'We see, in half-darkness, a large country house. We move past the house towards the paddocks, and as we move, so it grows lighter. We move into the stable-yards, and now it lightens into a cold, grey winter dawn . . . .'

SOME THIRTY YEARS AGO, Dylan Thomas was commissioned to write a film operetta for Gainsborough Pictures. *Me and My Bike* never progressed beyond the first twenty pages, but Dylan, taking to heart Thackeray's dictum 'Breakfast first, business next', began with a flourish:

Across the great hall of the manor house, a notably imposing butler walks, with gravity, to the foot of the huge curving stairs and blows on a hunting horn. From two doors at the far end of the hall come, in single file, two lines of servants, led by the massive and bombazined housekeeper. They take their places behind the butler and all look up the stairs. Down the stairs comes Sir Gregory Grig, fiercely moustached, ensanguined, vintage-portly, with poached eyes and mulberry nose. He is in riding kit, and carries a long whip in his hand.

"Good morning, Sir Gregory," says the butler.

"Mornin', Sir Gregory," says the housekeeper.

"Good morning, Sir Gregory Grig!" add the staff in unison.

And Sir Gregory, in acknowledgement of their greetings, cracks his whip. The staff disperses. Sir Gregory goes into the breakfast room. Here, the furniture is dark and elephantine. The enormous table, which could seat a hundred, is laid for four, acres of space between each place. All round the walls, where should be dark and heavy portraits of ancestors, are hung portraits of the heads of horses, painted in exactly the same style as would have been portraits of the ancestors. Sir Gregory goes to the sideboard, raises, one after the other, the covers of the huge silver dishes, commenting as he does so, in a rich North Country voice:

"York ham. Cold pheasant. Game pie. Lamb chops. Devilled kidneys. Curried eggs. Kedgeree." He shakes his head. "Pot luck again!"

He rakes a generous helping of each on to his great silver plate and goes down the sideboard to an array of bottles. He examines them, screwing up one eye. Claret. He turns away contemptuously.

"Boy's stuff. Brandy. Too early, damn it all. Burgundy. Remember what the vet said. Old ale it is."

A decoration by Leonora Box from the privately printed Me and My Bike *by Dylan Thomas, showing Sir Gregory Grig and his wife at breakfast*

Anyone who knew Dylan Thomas — as I [J. R.] did, in my capacity of scenario editor — soon realised that he was considerably more than the inspired and wayward poet of popular mythology and that anything he wrote was based on wide reading. This passage obviously owes a great deal to Surtees — of whom more later in connection with hunting breakfasts — but to what extent has he embroidered? The short answer, as will soon appear from actual menus and recipes printed by Major L . . . and 'Wyvern', is very little; but there were, in fact, wide variations in the scale of breakfast eaten during the eighteenth and nineteenth centuries.

The Reverend James Woodforde, who spent most of his life at a country parsonage at Weston Longueville in Norfolk, left a diary covering nearly every single day of the long stretch of years from 1758 to 1803. In it, he mentions almost every meal which he ate over the period, if only to say: 'I breakfasted, supped and slept again at the Parsonage.' More elaborate repasts are described in meticulous detail. By present-day standards, Woodforde, his niece and companion Nancy, his fellow clergymen the Rev. Thomas du Quesne and the Rev. Thomas Jeanes, and his friend Squire Custance, would seem huge trenchermen and copious drinkers, but were in all probability typical of their period.

To quote at random, on Wednesday, December 15, 1790, dinner for four guests, served at about 4 p.m., consisted of 'a couple of chicken boiled and a Ham, the best part of a large Rump of beef boiled, a plumb Pudding, a very fine fat Turkey, rosted Tarts &c.' After tea and quadrille, 'We gave our Company for Supper a rost Duck, some rosted Potatoes, Artichokes, Red Herrings, Hashed Turkey, Tarts &c. It was after

'The Curate's Egg' (from Punch, *1895)*

TRUE HUMILITY

Right Reverend Host. "I'M AFRAID YOU'VE GOT A BAD EGG, MR JONES!"
The Curate. "OH NO, MY LORD, I ASSURE YOU! PARTS OF IT ARE EXCELLENT!"

12. o'clock before I got to bed.' Dinner at Honingham Hall on November 7, 1786 was even more elaborate, consisting of 'some fine Soals, Soup, a Saddle of Mutton rosted, Tongue and boiled Turkey, some Patties and some Stakes — 2nd Course a Pheasant, Apple Pye, a fine Hare, Amulet, Blamange, Maccaroni, and some Eggs on Something.' Woodforde further notes, with some surprise, that there was 'No Desert whatever after Dinner', but that it was at least accompanied by 'Port, Cherry, Madeira, and Champaigne.'

Whether on account of these large dinners and suppers or because of his regular pint of port, Woodforde was much afflicted by gout in his later years and, despite an evening draught of rhubarb and ginger laced with rum, often awoke out of sorts. His appetite did not revive until later in the day, and it seems that he was a light breakfaster. One gathers that breakfast usually consisted of tea or coffee and toast, and if he specifies what he ate, it is usually when there was a journey in prospect, as on April 8 1784, when 'I got up this morning a little after 6 eat some cold Meat and drank half a Pint of small Beer — then mounted my Mare and went off for Norwich', or on April 4, 1786, when 'We breakfasted at the Kings Head at Beccles on Oysters and Tea and bread and butter and a very hearty breakfast we made, we then mounted our Horses and went on for Southwold....'

For detailed coverage of the English country-house breakfast in its full splendour one cannot do better than refer to the book by Major L... already mentioned and published a century later.

The Major writes with unfailing competence and scrupulous attention to detail and begins by classifying his subject matter:

1   Breakfasts for Large Parties
2   Breakfasts for Ladies and Men of Sedentary Habits and Pursuits
3   Breakfasts for Sportsmen and those of Active Habits

He next observes that 'in a country house, which contains, probably, a sprinkling of good and bad appetites and digestions, breakfasts should consist of a variety to suit all tastes, viz: fish, poultry, or game, if in season; sausages, and one meat of some sort, such as mutton cutlets, or fillets of beef; omelettes, and eggs served in a variety of ways; bread of both kinds, white and brown, and fancy bread of as many kinds as can conveniently be served; two or three kinds of jam, orange marmalade, and fruits when in season; and on the side table, cold meats such as ham, tongue, cold game, or game pie, galantines, and in winter a round of spiced beef of Mr Degue of Derby.'

But no cook can serve food at its best unless people are punctual, and the Major therefore recommends that the bill of fare should be sent up to the guests in their rooms and that each should name his choice and time, 'as at a club or military mess'. In this, with military gallantry, he particularly has the ladies in mind. 'Many ... will remember how frequently they have schemed to avoid sitting out so long a meal; how they have had to put up with everything being cold by coming down very late, and to make every excuse, except the true one for putting in so late an appearance.'

Those were the days of the 1d. post, when letters were delivered several times a day and on Sundays with the utmost promptitude; and the Major's second reason why 'the meal should not unnecessarily be prolonged, is, that the post in the country generally comes in about this time, and if letters require replies, every minute is of consequence to those who are going out on business or pleasure'.

With this introduction and a reminder that tea, coffee and cocoa, and the usual assortment of breads, toasts, muffins, preserves and fruit should

'A Country Breakfast' (contemporary nineteenth-century print)

be served with every breakfast, Major L... prints menus suitable for large parties for every month in the year. Here are his suggestions for February:

Kedgeree of Cod
Devilled Pheasant à la Perry
Broiled Ham
Mutton Chops
Eggs aux Fine Herbes

⬦———⬦

Broiled Haddock
Omelette aux Fine Herbes
Calf's Liver and Bacon
Mutton Cutlets
Eggs

⬦———⬦

Bloaters
Buttered Eggs aux Crevettes
Sausages aux Pommes
Devilled Pheasant
Poached Eggs and Bacon

⬦———⬦

Broiled Sole
Kidney Omelette
Hashed Mutton
Broiled Chicken, and Ham and Eggs
Eggs

⬦———⬦

COLD MEATS ON SIDE TABLE
Pheasants. Ham. Tongue. Galantine of
Guinea Fowl in Aspic. Spiced Round of Beef.

Ever mindful of the ladies, with whom he brackets 'Gentlemen of Sedentary occupation and of a Certain Age', the Major next proceeds to a selection of simplified menus.

'Ladies', as he explains, 'are as a rule much wiser, much more abstemious, and capable of practising much more self-denial in the feeding business than the male sex; the Author frequently admires the way in which they pass dish after dish, which men seldom, very seldom have the wisdom or strength of mind to pass; they rarely, too, eat meat for breakfast. He thinks, therefore, that it is wiser and kinder to put the men out of temptation, and although he may raise a hornets' nest about his ears he must say that men who take no exercise, or who are over fifty years of age, should, if they wish to preserve their health, and to avoid what the Author is told is not a particularly pleasant pain to endure, viz. the gout, never eat more than once a day; and *for this reason* he strongly advises them to adhere to the sort of breakfasts he recommends, and join the ladies in their abstemiousness and self-denial.'

Some twenty menus follow, again to be supplemented with breads, preserves and fruit, of which those shown below are typical: it will be

Broiled Salmon
Roast Larks
Eggs

⬦━━━⬦

Broiled Mackerel
Prawns
Broiled Duckling
Eggs

⬦━━━⬦

Turbot au Gratin
Buttered Eggs aux Pointes d'Asperges
Broiled Ham

⬦━━━⬦

Fried Smelt
Buttered Eggs and Purée of Haddock
Sausages

◆━━━◆

Broiled Haddock
Broiled Partridge
Buttered Eggs aux Truffes

◆━━━◆

COLD MEATS ON SIDE TABLE
Ham. Tongue. Poultry. Game Pies.
Galantines. Ballotines. Brawn.
Plovers' Eggs. Game.

noticed that, in spite of his good advice, the Major is fairly elastic over what does, and does not, constitute meat. No such pettifogging restrictions apply to this third type of breakfaster: 'People of Robust Constitution, Sportsmen, and Those who Take Much Exercise.'

Of 'such fortunate classes', Major L... observes that 'it matters little what they eat or drink, if their digestion is as good as their appetites', but he does strongly recommend tea, coffee or cocoa, rather than claret or beer, and draws the line at apple tart, washed down by 'home-brewed ale', a favourite of 'the late Sir Tatton Sykes'. With 'the greatest respect for the memory of this most worthy and excellent of baronets, he [the author] has not put such a Bill of Fare amongst his menus. Any one caring to try such a breakfast must cater for himself.'

The menus that follow resemble those of his first group, for example:

Fried Sole
Sauté of Kidneys
Devilled Chicken
Broiled Ham
Poached Eggs à la Creme

31

One suspects that, at this point in his book, Major L... was anxious to move on to his *pièce de résistance*, the chapter on 'Ball Suppers', where the menus are so lengthy and elaborate that he limits himself to four, tersely remarking that 'Any one who gives *more* than *four* balls in one year will probably be in a lunatic asylum before the next, so will not require more.'

Major L... backs up his menus with recipes for all the dishes that he mentions, some of which we reproduce, adjusting the quantities to four persons.

Less ambitious in scope, and therefore of more direct practical interest to today's breakfaster, is Colonel A. Kenney-Herbert's *Fifty Breakfasts*, published a few years later, in 1894. 'Wyvern', as he styles himself, dispenses with the cold meats on the side table and begins by saying that 'These little breakfast *menus* are designed for a family or party of six: each will be found to contain a dish of fish, a meat dish, and a dish of eggs, any two of which can be selected if three be considered too many,' and adds that 'Seven of them are composed for days of abstinence.'

'Wyvern' recommends 'tasty *rechauffés* of fish and meat' and suggests that the cook part-prepares 'these nice little dishes for breakfast' the previous evening. 'The "stitch in time" accomplished during the afternoon or before the kitchen fire is let down at night "saves nine" at the busy hour before breakfast next day. Indeed the ding-dong monotony of "bacon and eggs" alternated with "eggs and bacon" of many English breakfast tables is wholly inexcusable, so easy is it to provide variety with the exercise of a little consideration.'

Decorations from Mrs Beeton's Everyday Cookery, *1894* (below and right)

The nub is that today's cook is probably a harrassed housewife, perhaps with a job of her own, and unenthusiastic about cooking *anything* for breakfast. Nevertheless, some of 'Wyvern's' recipes, such as his minced ham on fried toast topped by a poached egg (recipe page 88), are simple to make and attractive, if only for a Sunday-morning spread or a light supper.

In the country houses in which we have occasionally stayed, Dylan Thomas's 'elephantine furniture' and tables the size of a tennis court still remain, together with other amenities, such as the revolving fire at Barmoor Castle in Berwickshire for heating either the library or the elegant oval morning room used for hunting breakfasts — but without, alas, the 'bombazined housekeeper' and lines of servants. Their gargantuan breakfasts survived throughout Edwardian times until the 1914 War and set the style for the elaborate repasts served on the Cunarders and other ocean-going liners during the twenties and thirties (see Chapter V). As a child, Humphrey Lyttleton, quoted by Ralph Pomeroy in *First Things First*, recalls a stately home where 'the Edwardian style still prevailed. Innumerable silver dishes were lined up on a hot plate, offering a staggering choice as one moved along them raising the lids. Eggs boiled, scrambled or fried, bacon, ham, kidney, huge flapping field mushrooms, sausages, kippers, haddock, sometimes even a cheese soufflé, and kedgeree . . . .'

But, in the main, such breakfasts are now only to be found in houses whose hard-pressed owners have taken to entertaining house-parties of wealthy Americans — for whom they remain as much a part of the traditional England as the Household Cavalry in their burnished helmets and scarlet uniforms.

Perhaps, on grounds of health, their passing is not entirely to be deplored. In Spain, there is a phrase 'eating with your eyes'; and this may well be a case where the shadow is preferable to the substance.

BACON, HAM AND SAUSAGES

Bacon was the old French name for pig and was used as such by Shakespeare, but nowadays it refers only to the back and sides of a pig after they have been cured and smoked. There are some ten different 'cuts' of bacon, but it is only the prime back and streaky which appear at breakfast, the others being mostly used for boiling.

Bacon may be grilled or fried and served by itself, but is nicer with such things as grilled tomatoes, sautéed kidneys or fried eggs, mushrooms, sliced black pudding or bread. Probably the best way of serving it is to grill it, so removing surplus fat. Arrange the rashers on the grill so that they overlap like slates on a roof with all the rinds exposed to the flame. In this way, the rinds will become crisp and edible, and the lean is shielded and well-basted until such time as the fat is thoroughly cooked. At this point it loses its transparency.

When frying bacon, do not add fat, but first cut off and fry the rinds, which will supply enough fat to cook the rashers themselves. One method is to tilt the pan, to cook the first rasher at the end furthest from the handle, and to move it up when done to make room for the next. By the time all the rashers have been cooked and moved up, there will be sufficient bacon fat at the bottom to fry the eggs.

Gammon of Ham

Gammon, a 'mild' ham made by curing the leg of the pig on the side before it is cut off the carcass, goes excellently with fried eggs when thickly sliced. It is juicier when fried, since it requires more cooking than thin rashers of bacon and tends to become dry when grilled.

HAM

Cold joints on the side table were a regular feature of the more elaborate Victorian breakfasts, and a slice or two of cold ham is as acceptable at breakfast as ever it was.

Among the different varieties of English ham are:

York Ham   Firm yet tender, with its attractive pink meat, it owes its mild flavour to the bracing airs of York and its Dry Salt Cure.

Bradenham Ham   A Wiltshire ham, made since 1781 by the Bradenham Ham Company of Chippenham by a special sweet and mild cure. The hams are hung for many months to mature and are recognizable by their coal-black outside.

Wiltshire Ham   This is, technically speaking, gammon. Mild and delicate in flavour, it is lightly cured and does not keep for as long as other hams.

Suffolk Ham   Fully-flavoured, with a degree of sweetness resulting from a special cure and long maturing.

Epicure Ham   The registered name of hams cured by the Epicure Ham Company of Pershore, Worcestershire, by an old and well-tried family recipe.

Hams should be soaked before cooking to remove excessive salt, either overnight in cold water or by standing in cold water for an hour or two and then gently bringing to the boil and discarding the liquid.

They may then be boiled, or rather simmered, for 25–30 minutes per lb. according to the thickness of the joint; but to seal in all the flavour it is perhaps preferable to wrap them in cooking foil and to bake in a moderate pre-heated oven (350°F, 180°C, Mark 4) for a similar period.

Here is an attractive recipe for glazed roast gammon, reproduced by courtesy of Frank Cooper's Oxford Marmalade:

Glazed Roast Gammon

2-3 lb (900 g-1½ kg) corner or middle gammon
3-4 tablespoons Frank Cooper's Coarse Cut 'Oxford' Marmalade

2 tablespoons demerara sugar

Weigh the piece of gammon and calculate the cooking time as twenty minutes per lb (450 g) plus twenty minutes over. Place the gammon in a large bowl and cover with cold water. Leave to stand overnight. Replace the soaking water with fresh, bring to the boil and simmer gently for about half of the cooking time. Remove from the heat and drain off the water (this could be used for making soup). Place the gammon in a roasting tin and remove the skin. Pour in just sufficient water to cover the base of the tin. Mix together the marmalade and the sugar and spread thickly over the gammon. Roast at 375°F (190°C) Mark 5 for the remainder of the cooking time.

SAUSAGES

Sausages are of two kinds, cooked and raw. The great institution, the English pork sausage, must, of course, be cooked before eating and goes particularly well with grilled bacon, fried mushrooms or grilled tomatoes — the acidity of the tomato contrasting well with the fattiness and richness of the sausage.

Pork sausages may be grilled or baked in the oven, but are at their most succulent when fried. First prick the skins to avoid their bursting and fry them in shallow fat or cooking oil at moderate heat, turning them from time to time, so as to brown the skin all over. Cooking time is about twenty minutes or ten minutes for the small chipolatas.

Few people now go to the trouble of making their own sausages, but here, as a matter of interest, is a recipe for making 'Oxford Sausages' from F. Marian McNeill's *Book of Breakfasts*:

1 lb (450g) young pork, fat and lean	*Nutmeg*
	6 sage leaves
1 lb (450g) lean veal	*Thyme*
1 lb (450g) beef suet	*Savory*
½ lb (225g) breadcrumbs	*Marjoram*
1 lemon	*Salt and pepper*

Take a pound of young pork, fat and lean, a pound of lean veal, and a pound of beef suet, remove all skin and gristle, and put them all through the mincer or chop very finely. Add half a pound of breadcrumbs. Shred half the rind of a lemon, grate half a nutmeg, chop finely six fresh sage leaves with a little thyme, savoury and marjoram, and add all these to the meat. Season with a teaspoonful of pepper and salt. Mix all well together and press down in a pan till required.

Flour the hands, and shape the sausage meat into rolls the size and shape of ordinary sausages. Fry in clarified fat, or cook under the grill.

Black Puddings

The Scots Black Puddings, blood sausages made with oatmeal, onion and spices, are best bought from the butcher. Somewhat similar to the Spanish *Morcilla*, they are delicious when fried in thin slices and served with bacon and eggs.

CHAPTER III

In Mr Surtees' Country

'Hurry up, hurry up, sleepy head
The horses used to say
Rubbing and tubbing it like a lord
And taking all the day
Hurry up, hurry up, sleepy Fred
Jump in your boots and jig!
If you don't come soon with our oats and bran
We'll tell Sir Gregory Grig!'
                    Dylan Thomas

O F THE BREAKFASTS served in country houses, hunt breakfasts differed from others and are a study in themselves. The form in late Victorian times is set out with admirable clarity in the anonymous *Party-Giving on Every Scale*, published in 1882.

A Hunt Breakfast partakes of the character of a cold luncheon on a large scale ... These breakfasts are given ... by the master of hounds, by the members of the hunt, or by any country gentleman near whose residence the meet takes place ... No invitations are issued for these breakfasts beyond those contained in the general notice given by the M. F. H. [Master of Fox Hounds] respecting the meets of the current week.

These breakfasts are given at the expense of the host of the day, and are entirely apart from the expenses of the hunt. The guests generally average forty to one hundred, including members of the hunt, residents and strangers.

The breakfast is given in the large dining-room, great hall, or billiard room, according to the accommodation required, one long table occupying the centre of the room. Breakfast covers are placed the length of the table; a knife and fork and plate to each cover, and as each place is vacated a fresh cover is placed in readiness for a new comer. Ladies are seldom present at hunt breakfasts, and those who ride or drive to the meet, and are acquainted with the lady of the house ... are ushered on their arrival into the drawing room or morning-room, where refreshments are offered to them, tea, coffee, sherry, sandwiches, cake etc.

9.30 to 10 is the time usually fixed for a hunt breakfast, although this is regulated by the hour at which the hounds are to meet. At hunt breakfasts hot entrées are not given; a large supply of cold viands is necessary; cold beef is the *pièce de résistance* at these entertainments, as the hunting farmers prefer something substantial to commence upon.

Twenty to thirty lbs. of sirloin or corned beef is usually provided ... Cold roast pheasant or game pie; roast chicken or roast turkey would also be given; and as this game or poultry would be furnished from the home preserves and home farm, the cost would be considerably under market price.

A piece of cheese, weighing from 12 lbs. to 15 lbs. .... either Cheddar or North Wiltshire ... bread and cheese is in great demand at hunt breakfasts.

All the cold meats, game, etc. are placed on the breakfast table, and the guests help themselves ... As a rule gentlemen eat but little at hunt breakfasts, and breakfast at home before starting; farmers, on the contrary, make a hearty meal, having perhaps breakfasted at a much earlier hour. A host, when ordering a hunt breakfast, takes into consideration the class of guests he expects, and regulates the supply according to the probable demand.

Sherry, brandy, cherry-brandy, liqueurs, and ale are always provided. Champagne is only occasionally given.

Owing to a hasty and often less than usually abundant breakfast, many a hunting gentleman found himself decidedly peckish before the morning was out; and the prescient Major L ... makes a telling comment: 'In hunting counties the Author has frequently heard the remarks: "What can we take with us for lunch; which sandwich is the best; should it be made of bread or toast; or, What is the best meat to use?" He can also hear others exclaiming: "What is the man thinking about? *We* don't want to eat out hunting; *We* can't be bothered by carrying packages; We hate our saddles turned into pack-saddles," etc. Wait, my friends, until the

'Breakfast and Tea China', from Mrs Beeton's Everyday Cookery, *1894*

clock of some neighbouring village strikes two, and you see a friend produce a pie full of jelly, or a cutlet covered with aspic, made by the receipts given in this book.'

One finds the odd comment on breakfast foods sprinkled through the literature of hunting (for example, in Somerville and Ross's inimitable *Experiences of an Irish R.M.*, their hero 'kept to himself' his 'long-formed opinion that eating pollock was like eating boiled cotton wool with pins in it') but, when all is said and done, the most satisfactory descriptions of hunting breakfasts, among the most vivid of food in any English novels, are those of Robert Smith Surtees from *Jorrocks' Jaunts and Jollities* and *Mr Sponge's Sporting Tour*.

So, 'the sign of the "Greyhound"'... greets the expectant optics' of the converging sportsmen. 'The bustle increases; sportsmen arrive by the score, fresh tables are laid out, covered with "no end" of vivers; and towards the hour of nine, may be heard to perfection, that pleasing assemblage of sounds issuing from the masticatory organs of a number of men steadfastly and studiously employed in the delightful occupation of preparing their mouthfuls for deglutition. "O noctes coenaeque Deum," said friend Flaccus. Oh, hunting breakfasts! say we. Where are now the jocund laugh, the oft-repeated tale, the last debate? As our sporting contemporary, the *Quarterly*, said, when describing the noiseless pursuit of old reynard by the Quorn: "Reader, there is no crash now, and not much music." It is the tinker who makes a great noise over a little work, but, at the pace these men are eating, there is no time for babbling. So, gentle lector, there is now no leisure for the bandying of compliments, 'tis your small eater alone who chatters over his meals; your true-born sportsman is ever silent and, consequently, an assiduous grubber. True it is that occasionally space is found between mouthfuls to vociferate "WAITER!" in a tone that does not require repetition; and sonorously do the throats of the assembled eaters re-echo the sound; but this is all — no useless exuberance of speech — no, the knife or fork is directed towards what is wanted, nor needs there any more expressive intimation of the applicant's wants.'

Though both were great trenchermen and shared a common passion for hunting, Soapey Sponge and Mr Jorrocks were in other respects very different. The impecunious Mr Sponge, a 'good-looking, rather vulgar-looking man' with 'groomy gait and horsey propensities' early hit on an ingenious device for indulging his ruling passion. From a dubious horse-dealer and on easy terms, he acquired the redoubtable Hercules, described by its vendor, Buckram, as 'an oss in hevery respect werry like your work, but he's an oss I'll candidly state, I wouldn't put in every one's 'ands, for, in the fust place, he's wery walueous, and in the second he requires an ossman to ride.' In Sponge's expert hands, the vicious Hercules was always the first in at the kill; Sponge would then peddle him for a few hundred guineas to a follower of the local hunt, who, on the adventitious arrival of the unscrupulous Buckram a week or two later, would be glad to dispose of the brute on any terms.

In this manner and by cadging free accommodation on the strength of his undoubted abilities in the field, Sponge duped a whole series of unsuspecting sportsmen, beginning with Mr Waffles of the Laverick Wells Hunt and continuing with Mr Jawleyford of Jawleyford Court, Lord Scamperdown, Mr Puffington, Mr Jogglebury Crowdey and Mr Facey Romford — to mention only a few — living and eating at their expense.

As a breakfaster, Sponge was somewhat perfunctory, in his anxiety to be at the meet in time. At Jawleyford Court, for example, 'it was a quarter to nine ere Spigot [the butler] appeared with the massive silver urn, followed by the train-band bold, bearing the heavy implements of breakfast . . . so it was nearly nine before Mr Sponge got his fork into his first mutton chop. Jawleyford was not exactly pleased; he thought it didn't look well for a young man to prefer hunting to the society of his lovely and accomplished daughters . . . .

' "You'll have a fine day, my dear Mr Sponge," said he, extending a hand, as he found our friend brown-booted and red-coated, working away at the breakfast.

' "Yes," said Sponge, munching away for hard life. In less than ten minutes, he managed to get as much down, as with the aid of a notch of bread that he pocketed, he thought would last him through the day . . . .'

As the guest of Mr Jogglebury Crowdey at Puddingpote Bower, Sponge suffered even more distraction in the shape of an infant prodigy given to recitation:

> "Bah, bah, black sheep, have 'ou any 'ool?
> Ess, marry, have I, three bags full;
> Un for ye master, un for ye dame.
> Un for ye 'ittle boy 'ot 'uns about ye 'ane."

'Mr Sponge's Rapid Breakfast' at Jawleyford Court (drawing by John Leech from Mr Sponge's Sporting Tour*)*

But unfortunately, Mr Sponge was busy with his breakfast, and the prodigy wasted his sweetness on the desert air....

'"A little more (puff) tea, my (wheeze) dear," said Jogglebury, thrusting his great cup up the table.

'"Hush! Jog, hush!" exclaimed Mrs Crowdey, holding up her forefinger, and looking significantly first at him and then at the urchin.

'With more prompting Gustavus James responded with:

> "Diddle, diddle, doubt,
> My candle's out,
> My 'ittle dame's not at 'ome —
> So saddle my hog, and bridle my dog
> And bring my 'ittle dame 'ome...."

'Mrs Jog was delighted, and found herself pouring the tea into the sugar-basin instead of into Jog's cup.

'Mr Sponge, too, applauded. "Well, that *was* very clever," said he, filling his mouth with cold ham. "Saddle my dog, and bridle my hog — I'll trouble you for another cup of tea," addressing Mrs Crowdey.

'"No, not saddle my dog, sil-l-e-y man!" drawled the child, making a pet lip: "saddle my *hog*."

'"Oh! saddle my hog, was it?" replied Mr Sponge, with apparent surprise: "I thought it was saddle my dog. I'll trouble you for the

'The Domestic Economy of Nonsuch House' (*from* Mr Sponge's Sporting Tour)

42

'The Sponge Cigar and Betting Rooms' (from Mr Sponge's Sporting Tour*)*

sugar, Mrs Jogglebury", adding, "you have devilish good cream here; how many cows have you?"'

On dropping in for an early breakfast at Nonsuch House, the seat of the profligate Sir Harry Scatterdash, Mr Sponge found the domestic economy in even greater disorder. 'The last waxlight was just dying out in the centre of a splendid candelabra on the middle of a table scattered about with claret-jugs, glasses, decanters, pine-apple tops, grape-dishes, cakes, anchovy-toast plates, devilled biscuit-racks — all the concomitants of a sumptuous entertainment,' and on enquiring of the slatternly maid for breakfast — 'just some coffee and a mutton chop or two' — he was summarily turned down and informed that the butler, Mr Bottleends, was not to be disturbed until the following day. However, his visit to Nonsuch House was to turn out for the best, since it was here that he met 'the beautiful and tolerably virtuous Miss Glitters of Astley's Royal Amphitheatre', whom in due course he married and with whose help he fitted up and decorated 'the splendid establishment in Jermyn Street, St James's, now known as the SPONGE CIGAR AND BETTING ROOMS.'

Mr Jorrocks, an ardent follower of the Surrey Hunt, was fonder of his creature comforts and more of a gastronome than Mr Sponge, as will appear from the account of his visit to France in Chapter VI. This was perhaps to be expected, as he was 'a substantial grocer in St Botolph's Lane, with an elegant residence in Great Coram Street, Russell Square.' Surtees describes him as 'a cockney sportsman . . . a very excellent fellow — frank, hearty, open, generous and hospitable, and with the exception of riding up Fleet Street one Saturday afternoon, with a cock-pheasant's tail sticking out of his red coat pocket, no one ever saw him do a cock-tail action in his life.'

During a visit to take the waters at Cheltenham — 'though altogether opposed to the element, he not having "astonished his stomach", as he says, for the last fifteen years with a glass of water,' — he picked up so rapidly 'after a few good drenches' that 'to whatever inn they went to dine, the landlords and waiters were astounded at the consumption of prog., and in a very short time he was known from the Royal Hotel down to the Hurlston's Commercial Inn, as the great London Cormorant.'

A breakfast offered at Great Coram Street to a young Yorkshireman, his inseparable companion on his adventures in the field and dining room, is probably the most elaborate to be described in English literature:

It was a nice comfortable-looking place with a blazing fire, half the floor covered with an old oil-cloth, and the rest exhibiting the cheerless aspect of naked flags. About a yard and a half from the fire was placed the breakfast table; in the centre stood a magnificent uncut ham, with a great quartern loaf on one side and a huge Bologna sausage on the other; besides these there were nine eggs, two pyramids of muffins, and a great deal of toast, a dozen ship-biscuits, and half a pork pie, while a dozen kidneys were spluttering on a spit before the fire, and Betsy held a gridiron covered with mutton chops on the top; altogether there were as much as would have served ten people. "Now, sit down," said Jorrocks, "and let us be doing, for I am as hungry as a hunter. Hope you are peckish too; what shall I give you? tea or coffee? — but take both — coffee first and tea after a bit. If I can't give them to you good, don't know who can. You must pay your devours, as we say in France, to the 'am, for it is an expecial fine one, and do take a few eggs with it; there, I've not given you above a pound of 'am, but you can come again, you know — 'waste not want not'. Now take some muffins, do, pray. Betsy, bring some more cream, and set the kidneys on the table, the Yorkshireman is getting nothing to eat. Have a chop with your kidneys, werry luxurious — I could eat an elephant stuffed with grenadiers, and wash them down with an ocean of tea; but pray lay into the breakfast, or I shall think you don't like it. There, now take some tea and toast or one of those biscuits, or whatever you like; wouldn't a little more 'am be agreeable? Batsey, run into the larder and see if your Missis left any of that cold chine of pork last night — and hear, bring the cold goose, and any cold flesh you can lay hands on, there are really no wittles on the table. I am quite ashamed to set you down to such a scanty fork breakfast; but this is what comes of not being master of your own house. Hope your hat may long cover your family; rely upon it, it is "cheaper to buy your bacon than to keep a pig."

At this point they were interrupted by an indignant Mrs Jorrocks, 'her hair tucked up in papers and a pair of worsted slippers on her feet', who rounded on her husband with, "What is the meaning of this card? I found it in your best coat pocket, which you had on last night."' The Yorkshire-man, unwillingly involved, muttered: "'It is the night he usually spends at the "Magpie and Stump", but whether he was there or not I cannot pretend to say . . . ." "There, then, take it and read it," interrupted Mrs J.; — and he took the card accordingly — a delicate pale pink, with blue borders and gilt edge — and read — we would fain put in dashes and asterisks — "Miss Juliana Granville, John Street, Waterloo Road . . . .'"

Jorrocks was fortunately rescued by the arrival of 'a monstrous nice carriage' to carry them to the meet of the Surrey Staghounds . . . .

Though this was perhaps Surtees' *pièce de résistance*, we have only scratched the surface of the many memorable breakfast scenes scattered through his books.

There was, for example, that satisfying breakfast at the lawn meet of the Larkspur at Rosemont Grange 'conducted pretty much on the London Club principle, each guest having his separate *ménage* — viz., two teapots containing the beverage, the other hot water, a small glass basin of sugar, a ditto butter-boat and cream ewer, together with a muffin or bun, and a rack of dry toast. A common coffee-pot occupied the centre of the round-table, flanked on the one side with a well-filled egg-stand, and on the other with a beautiful dish of moor-edge honey. On the side table were hot meats and cold, with the well-made household bread. Hence each man, on coming down, rang for his own supply without reference to any one else — a great convenience to fox-hunters, who like riding leisurely on instead of going full tilt to cover.'

We encounter Facey Romford, Master of Fox Hounds, at another house in the Larkspur country, where his companion, Mrs Somerville 'was downstairs already, but not in her sporting costume, it being one of her rules, when alone, always to put on her smart things after breakfast, considering that they ran more risk of damage at that meal than during all the rest of the day put together. Lucy was only a light breakfast eater, Facey a heavy one — a little dry toast, a cup of tea, and an egg sufficing for her, while our master indulged in oatmeal porridge, pork chops, rabbit pieces, cold game — the general produce of his gun, in fact.'

There were disappointments, it is true, as at the meet of the Duke of Tergiversation's hounds, where 'there was no hospitality used, not even a horn of ale or a bit of bread and cheese'. But the Duke was notoriously a munificent supporter of the chase in everything except the main essentials, and such setbacks were rare.

We take leave of Mr Sponge, Mr Jorrocks, Facey Romford and the others, munching their way through muffins and mutton chops to all eternity....

MEAT AND GAME

Mutton Chops
Of all the hearty traditional English breakfast dishes, mutton chops were perhaps the favourite, though they rarely appear on the breakfast-table today; and mutton, the flesh of a sheep from one to five years old, has largely been displaced from the butchers by lamb.

In Victorian times they were generally broiled on the spit over an open fire. Nowadays they are usually cooked under the grill in the usual way for 8-10 minutes on each side, the meat first being sealed to retain the juices and flavour by two minutes' cooking on either side under a high flame.

The Earl of Howth's Devilled Kidneys
Devilled kidneys were another Victorian favourite in large country houses. This simple recipe is adapted from André Simon's *Concise Encyclopaedia of Gastronomy*:

2 lb (900 g) lambs' kidneys	1 teaspoon dry mustard
1 tablespoon vinegar	1 dessertspoon Worcestershire Sauce
1 oz (30 g) butter	

First wash the kidneys and soak them for an hour in cold water and vinegar. Drain and rinse, remove skin and membranes, and split. Shake a little seasoning inside; sauté in a frying pan with butter for about ten minutes and pour the sauce around.

Hashed Lamb with Pickled Walnuts
For some reason hashed lamb and minced beef with pickled walnuts regularly appear on the breakfast menus of the old liners — one would hardly have thought them appropriate to stormy weather in the Atlantic! Here, at any rate, is a very savoury recipe adapted from Major L...'s *Breakfasts, Luncheons, and Ball Suppers*:

1 oz (30 g) butter	*¾ pint (450 ml) meat stock,*
8 oz (225 g) chopped onions	*or use cube*
1 tablespoon flour	*8 oz (225 g) remains of roast lamb,*
1 tablespoon chopped	*cut up*
parsley	*Squeeze of lemon juice*
2 pickled walnuts, chopped	*Salt and pepper*

Melt the butter in a frying pan and cook the chopped onion for ten minutes. Add the flour, chopped parsley, the finely chopped pickled walnuts and the stock, stir well together and simmer gently for fifteen minutes. Add the cut-up meat, squeeze in a little lemon juice, season with salt and pepper and heat together for a further fifteen minutes.

If preferred, you may first make the sauce and leave the meat to marinate in it before final heating and serving.

Breakfast Grill
That Queen of the Breakfast Table, F. Marian McNeill, advises that 'when a substantial breakfast dish is required a plain or mixed grill is particularly suitable'.

For a plain grill she recommends grilled chops, or mutton cutlets, fillet of beef, or rump steak (see instructions for grilling on page 46) and explains that a correct mixed grill 'consists of one or two mutton cutlets, one sheep kidney split in halves, two rashers of bacon and a sausage'. She adds that the dish is improved by garnishing it with grilled tomatoes and mushrooms and that it should be served with sauté potatoes (see page 77).

Purée of Game in Scallops
Game pies were also a feature of the groaning Victorian side-table. The

enthusiast should refer to the mouth-watering but elaborate recipe given in Major L . . .'s book, or with considerably less effort, repair to the food department of a well-known store in Knightsbridge.

The following recipe from 'Wyvern's' *Fifty Breakfasts* for Purée of Game in Scallops is simple and appetizing. Quantities will depend on the amount of left-over game available, and small fireproof dishes may be used in place of scallop shells.

Left-over game or turkey	*1 teaspoon redcurrant jelly*
Broth from the carcass	*1 dessertspoon Marsala or brown sherry*
Flour for thickening	*Breadcrumbs, salt and pepper*

Pick and mince the meat from the birds overnight, and make as much well-flavoured broth from the bones as you can. This having been prepared, the work next morning will be quickly done. Simply thicken the broth with flour, flavour it with Marsala [or cream sherry] and redcurrant jelly, season it with salt, and a teaspoonful of spiced pepper. Then stir in the mince, keep it hot in a *bain-marie* while you butter six scallop shells, into which, when ready, pour the mince, shake a layer of pounded breadcrumbs over the surface of each, and heat well in the oven; brown the crumbs [under the grill], and send up.

IRISH HOSPITALITY.

Sung with great Applause by Mr. INCLEDON, in his New Entertainment, called "THE MINSTREL."

[Tune—Town and Country.]

Assist me, ye lads, who have hearts free from guile,
To sing in the praise of old Ireland's isle;
Where true hospitality opens the door,
And friendship detains us for one bottle more.
      Fol de rol lol.

Old England, your taunts on our country forbear,
With our bulls and our brogues we are true and sincere;
For if but one bottle remains in our store,
We have generous hearts to give that bottle more.

At Candy's, in Church Street, I'll sing of a set
Of six Irish blades, who together had met;
Four bottles apiece made us call for the score,
And nothing detain'd us but one bottle more.

Our bill being paid, we were loth to depart,
For friendship had grappled each man by the heart;
Where the least touch, you know, makes an Irishman roar,
So a whack from shelali brought six bottles more.
      Fol de rol lol.

Now Phœbus had shone through our windows so bright,
Quite happy to view his blest children of light;
So we parted, with hearts neither sorry nor sore,
Resolving next night to drink twelve bottles more.

Published, the 20th October, 1815,

BY J. WHITTLE AND R. H. LAURIE,

NO. 53, FLEET STREET, LONDON.

'Irish Hospitality', 1815

'The Man of Taste', Thomas Rowlandson, 1789

'The Breakfast', Thomas Rowlandson, 1789

'Stage Coach Passengers at Breakfast', J. Pollard, c. 1830

'Eating at a Country Inn', J. Green (nineteenth-century print)

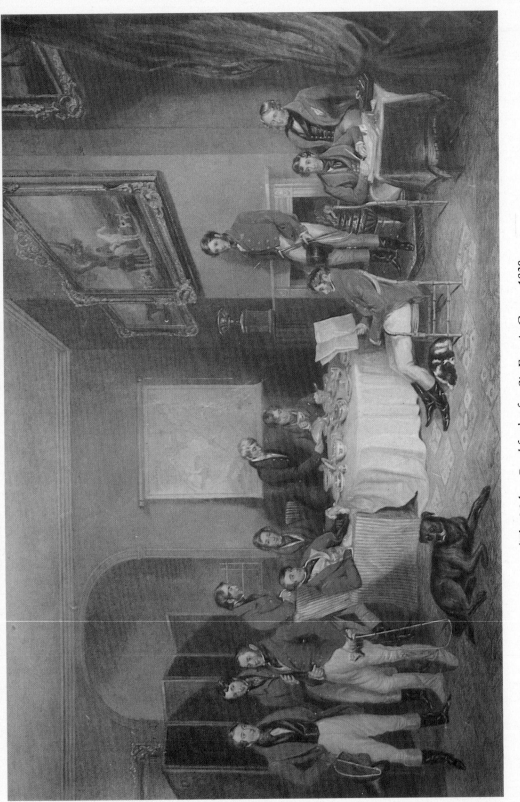

'The Melton Breakfast', after Sir Francis Grant, 1839

CHAPTER IV

The Scottish Breakfast

'In the breakfast, the Scots, whether of the Lowlands or mountains, must be confessed to excel us. The tea and coffee are accompanied not only with butter, but with honey, conserves and marmalades. If an epicure could remove by a wish in quest of sensual gratification, wherever he had supped, he would breakfast in Scotland.'
Dr Johnson, quoted in Boswell's *Tour of the Hebrides*

COMING FROM ONE who on other occasions remarked that 'the noblest prospect which a Scotchman ever sees, is the high road that leads him to England!' or 'Seeing Scotland, Madam, is only seeing a worse England', this is praise indeed. Tradition has not been allowed to lapse, and if the Great British Breakfast survives anywhere, it is in the hotels of the Highlands, especially those catering for the healthy appetites of fishermen, and in the more modest 'bed and breakfast' places along the way.

A Scots breakfast, as served in a Highland hotel, still sets one up for the day. When the menu lists boiled or fried eggs, it means what it says — eggs and not egg. Apart from porridge, eggs and bacon, grilled sausages and tomatoes, crisp fried bread and perhaps a slice or two of fried black pudding, there is a choice of smoked fish: oak-smoked kippers, Arbroath Smokies or Finnan haddock. And, in addition to toast, there are always oatcakes and 'morning rolls', fresh from the baker's oven.

Two of the staples of the breakfast table, orange marmalade, first made in Dundee in the eighteenth century (see Chapter VII), and porridge, are of Scots origin.

In her charming books, *The Scots Kitchen* and the *Book of Breakfasts*, F. Marian McNeill supplies a fund of information on the making of porridge (see recipe, page 76) and its early origins. A variant was the

Aigar (Oatmeal) Brose, made by stirring oatmeal and butter with boiling water. Supped with 'sour dook' (buttermilk) or sweet milk, it was, as Miss McNeill says, 'the backbone of many a sturdy Scotsman.'

There was a mystique about the preparation and consumption of porridge. The oatmeal was traditionally stirred into the boiling water sunwise, or with a right-hand turn, for luck, with a special porridge-stick known as a 'spurtle', 'theevil' or 'gruel-tree'. Porridge was traditionally eaten while standing and was habitually referred to in the plural as 'they'. According to differences in the making, it was variously called *brochan* in the Highlands, *bleirie* in Lanarkshire, *lewands* in Clydeside, *bluthrie* in Ettrick and Forfarshire, *gogar* in Roxburghshire and *whillins* in Fife, while a gruel made by beating the remains left at breakfast and adding fresh whey and oatmeal rejoiced in the name of *whey-whullions*.

Porridge was usually accompanied by porter or small beer, the 'Scotch drink' in the days of Robert Burns, hence his lines:

> On thee aft Scotland chows her cood,
> In souple scones, the wale o' food!
> Or tumblin' in the boiling flood
> > Wi' kail an' beef;
> But when thou pours thy strong heart's blood,
> > There thou shines chief...
>
> Aft, clad in massy siller weed,
> Wi' gentles thou erects they head;
> Yet, humbly kind in time o' need,
> > The poor man's wine;
> His wee drap parritch, or his bread,
> > Thou kitchens fine.

Among the better-to-do, porridge was only the foundation of a good breakfast, and in 1708 an English visitor, Chamberlayne, wrote that, 'The diet of the Scots is agreeable to their estates and qualities. No people eat better, or have greater varieties of flesh, fish, wild and tame fowl, than the Scots nobility and gentry in their own country, where they can furnish their tables with ten dishes cheaper than the English can provide three of the same kinds....'

A Frenchman, Bartolomé Faujas de Saint Fond, who toured Scotland in 1784, has left an interesting account* of how he fared at the great castles

---

* in *Travels in England and Scotland*, 1784

and houses of the Highlands. Thus he writes of a sojourn with the Duke of Argyll at Inverary Castle:

. . . Each person rose in the morning at any hour he pleased. Some took a ride, others went to the chase. I started off at sunrise to examine the natural history of the neighbourhood.

At ten o'clock a bell gives warning that it is breakfast-time: we then repair to a large room, ornamented with historical pictures of the family; among which there are some by Battoni, Reynolds and other eminent Italian and English painters. Here we find several tables, covered with tea-kettles, fresh cream, excellent butter, rolls of several kinds, and in the midst of all bouquets of flowers, newspapers, and books. There are besides, in this room, a billiard table, pianos and other musical instruments.

The main meal of the day, dinner, was at half-past four and 'is eaten with pleasure, for the dishes are prepared after the manner of an excellent French cook, every thing is served here as in Paris, except some courses in the English style, for which a certain predilection is preserved; but this

Inverary Castle, where Bartolomé Faujas de Saint Fond breakfasted with the Duke of Argyll in 1784

makes a variety, and thus gives the epicures of every country an opportunity of pleasing their palates.'

The ladies withdrew after dessert, while the gentlemen regaled themselves with port and champagne, finally rejoining them in the drawing-room for tea and coffee. Saint Fond adds that: 'At ten o'clock supper was served, and those attended it who pleased.' One gathers that there were few with the requisite stamina....

Breakfast at the house of Mr Maclean of Torloisk in Mull was more elaborate:

> ... At ten in the morning, the bell announces breakfast. All repair to the parlour, where they find a fire of peat mixed with pit-coal, and a table neatly served and covered with the following dishes:

Slices of smoked beef
Cheese of the country and English cheese, in
trays of mahogany
Fresh eggs
Hash of salted herring
Butter
Milk and cream
A sort of pap, of oatmeal and water (porridge).
In eating this thick pap, each spoonful is
plunged alternatively into cream, which is
always alongside.
Milk mingled with the yolks of eggs, sugar and
rum. This singular mixture is drunk cold and
without having been cooked.
Currant jelly
Conserve of myrtle, a wild fruit that grows on
the heaths (blaeberry jam)
Tea
Coffee
The three sorts of bread above-mentioned
Jamaica Rum

Such is the style in which Mr Maclean's breakfast table was served every morning, while we were at his house. There was always the same abundance, and I noticed in general no other difference than in the greater or less variety of the dishes.

Sir Walter Scott, who fostered a renaissance of Scots cooking (from a painting by Andrew Geddes, A.R.A.)

A ten-course dinner followed at 4 p.m., all the dishes appearing at the same time and the mistress of the house doing the honours; but this was not the end, for 'what is perhaps a little unpleasant, is that at ten o'clock one must again take one's seat at table and share until mid-night in a supper of nearly the same kind as the dinner, and in no less abundance.

'Such,' Saint Fond concludes, 'is the life that is led in a country where there is not a road nor a tree, where the mountains are covered only with heath, where it rains for eight months of the year, and where the sea, always in motion, seems to be in perpetual convulsions....'

One of the great exponents of the Scots cuisine was Sir Walter Scott. In *St Ronans Well* he celebrates the formation of the famous Cleikum Club, devoted to its revival; and somewhat later a Mrs Johnson, the wife of an Edinburgh publisher, borrowed the name of Meg Dods, at whose inn in the Borders the club met, to write the *Cook and Housewife's Manual*, a book of authentic Scots recipes which F. Marian McNeill unhesitatingly ranks with the contemporary *Physiologie du Goût* by Brillat-Savarin.

Scott himself was no mean breakfaster, as his biographer, Lockhart, reports: 'Breakfast was his chief meal. Before that came he had gone through the severest part of the day's work... His plate was always provided, in addition to the usual delicacies of a Scotch breakfast, with some solid article, on which he did most lusty execution — a round of beef — a pasty, such as made Gil Blas's eyes water — or, most welcome of all, a cold sheep's head, the charms of which primitive dainty he has so gallantly defended against the disparaging sneers of Dr Johnson and his bear-leader. A huge brown loaf flanked his elbow, and it was placed on a broad wood trencher that he might cut and come again with the bolder knife . . . He never ate anything more before dinner, and at dinner he ate sparingly.'

His novels abound in descriptions of breakfasts, written with all the gusto of the enthusiast. In *Waverley*, set in the eighteenth century, 'Waverley found Miss Bradwardine presiding over the tea and coffee, the table loaded with warm bread, both of flour, oatmeal and barleymeal, in the shape of loaves, cakes, biscuits, and other varieties, together with eggs, reindeer ham, mutton and beef ditto, smoked salmon, marmalade, and all the other delicacies which induced even Johnson himself to extol the luxury of a Scotch breakfast above that of all other countries. A mess of oatmeal porridge, flanked by a silver jug, which held an equal mixture of cream and milk, was placed for the Baron's share of this repast.'

And here is a charming description of an *al fresco* breakfast from the same book:

'Much nearer to the mouth of the cave he heard the notes of a lively Gaelic song, guided by which, in a sunny recess shaded by a glittering birch-tree, and carpeted with a bank of firm white sand, he found the damsel of the caravan, whose lay had already reached him, busy, to the best of her power, in arranging a morning repast of milk, eggs, barley bread, fresh butter and honeycomb . . . To this she now added a few bunches of cranberries, gathered in the adjacent morass . . . Evan and his attendant now returned slowly along the beach, the latter bearing a large salmon-trout, the produce of the morning's sport . . . A spark from the lock of his pistol produced a light, and a few withered fir branches were quickly in flame, and as speedily reduced to hot embers, on which the trout was broiled in large slices. To crown the repast, Evan produced from the pocket of his short jerkin a large scallop-shell, and from under the folds of his plaid a ram's horn full of whiskey. Of this he took a copious dram.'

I [J. R.] was lucky enough to be brought up in a country town in Scotland between the wars, in the days when there was still a maid to light a fire in the dining-room and to cook breakfast. Although our breakfasts were hardly on the scale of those just described, we began with fresh fruit, followed by porridge in winter or cereal in summer, continuing with bacon and eggs, perhaps served with fried bread, mushrooms or a slice or two of fried black pudding, and ending with toast and home-made marmalade. Oddly enough, on Sunday, breakfast was less elaborate and always consisted of boiled eggs; but Sundays, apart from lunch, were generally less formal — it was the one day of the week when one was not expected to change into evening dress for dinner.

In those days St Andrews still possessed an active fishing community and the boats went out from the harbour early every morning, returning in the late afternoon. The fresh fish was legion; and large crabs, regarded as vermin by the Scots, sold at 6d apiece. But it was the smoked fish from Aberdeen and Arbroath up the coast which appeared on the breakfast table, varying the normal regimen of bacon and eggs.

Kippers, not perhaps as large and juicy as those from Loch Fyne in the west, but smoked over oak chips in the traditional way instead of a hasty curing and incorporation of orange dye, were brought to the door by fishwives in striped blue and white aprons, who regularly took the train from Aberdeen to peddle their wares. In our early days there, I well remember my mother, a Yorkshirewoman, turning down a pressing offer of 'bony kippers', only to realise too late that the operative word was 'bonnie'.

Scots fisher-folk (contemporary nineteenth-century engraving)

Bloaters (see page 60) are not a Scots speciality, but Arbroath Smokies are equally delicious and, like bloaters, should be bought and eaten as fresh as possible. They are still cured in the sheds clustering the harbour of Arbroath, rather north of Dundee, by hanging up whole haddock in couples in a small brick kiln and lightly smoking them over smouldering hardwood chips.

Arbroath's other speciality is Finnan (or 'Finney') haddock, named after the hamlet of Findon in Kincardineshire, just north of Aberdeen. In this case, the haddock is split and smoked either on the bone or as 'golden fillets'. It makes an excellent breakfast or supper dish, especially when topped with a poached egg (see notes on serving up smoked fish, page 59).

Salmon and smoked salmon, now almost worth their weight in gold, are no longer much served for breakfast, except occasionally in fishing hotels in the Highlands, where brass scales are sometimes provided in the lobby for the returning fisherman to deposit his catch. As a boy, at school near Perth, I can remember those red-letter days when some angler parent would present a whole salmon to his son's 'house', and we would be given it hot for breakfast. Some of the best smoked salmon, incidentally, hails from Scott's Fish Shop in Kirkwall, 'capital' of Orkney, suppliers by Royal Warrant to Queen Elizabeth the Queen Mother, where much of it is smoked for private customers and first cured in rum and Demerara sugar according to a secret family recipe.

The small bakeries of such towns as Perth, Dundee and St Andrews, fragrant with the smell of fresh bread and spices, are unrivalled throughout the British Isles for their crusty loaves, milk bread, morning rolls, scones, baps, oatcakes, potato scones, shortbread, and profusion of biscuits, pastries and cakes. These things come into their own at the Scots 'high tea' (a survival of the old four o'clock dinner?) — less popular than it was, but still served at many 'bed and breakfast' places — where they are accompanied by a substantial meat or fish dish. Recipes for the morning rolls, oatcakes and potato scones eaten at breakfast are given on pages 86, 77 and 78. The potato scone (pronounced, be it noted, 'sconn' and not 'scoan') is much thinner than its tea-time namesake, more in fact of a pancake and quite different again from a potato cake, and is delicious when fried with bacon and mushrooms.

It must appear from all this that Scotland excels in breakfasts, and Dr

Opposite page: *A Leith fishwife (calotype by D. O. Hill)*

No. 36.

GRILLED SALMON.

Average cost of Ingredients.

	s.	d.
1½ lb. salmon (cut in two slices) 1/4 per lb. ...	2	0
2 oz. butter	0	2½
Pepper and salt		
Cayenne pepper	0	2
1 tablespoonful chopped capers		
	2	4½

Time required, about twenty minutes.

---

1. Wash the slices of *salmon* in fresh cold water, and wipe them dry with a cloth; take *two pieces of white paper*, *butter* them, and fold up each slice of *salmon* separately in the *buttered paper*.

2. Put the *salmon* on a gridiron, and grill it in front of a clear fire, for about *a quarter of an hour*. It must be turned frequently, or the paper will burn.

3. Put the rest of the *butter* on a plate, and mix with it *a saltspoonful of salt, half-a-saltspoonful of pepper*, and about *five grains of cayenne pepper;* then mix in the *capers*, which should be very finely chopped.

4. When the *salmon* is cooked, take off the paper; spread the *butter* and *capers* all over the fish, and serve it on a hot dish.

N.B.—If preferred, the slices of salmon could be dipped in egg and bread-crumbs and fried, and then served with the same butter, and some fried parsley.

A recipe for grilled salmon (from R.O.C.'s Breakfast and Savoury Dishes, 1885)

Johnson's advice is as sound now as when he delivered it it 1773. When Boswell first mooted the idea of touring the Hebrides, Voltaire 'looked at me, as if I had talked of going to the North Pole, and said, "You do not insist on my accompanying you?" — "No, sir." — "Then I am very willing you should go."'

One must grant that there were compensations.

FISH

One of the many delights of breakfasts in Scotland is the smoked fish, which is cooked very simply.

Arbroath Smokies

As already noted, smokies should be eaten as fresh as possible; even those from fishmongers in Scotland are not as delicate and full of flavour as the smokie bought fresh from the sheds in Arbroath. Smokies may be eaten cold, but benefit from heating.

Remove the heads and tails, place the smokies in about ½-inch of water in a large frying pan, cover and bring to the boil. Simmer for about ten minutes until they are really hot, turning them once, then remove with a slotted spoon and put on a hot plate. Split them down the middle and take out the backbone. Season with freshly-ground pepper, dot with butter, then close the fish and serve at once, since they cool quickly.

Kippers

To enjoy kippers at their succulent best, they should not, as so many Sassenachs think, be boiled in water. The traditional Scots method is to lay them face to face in a frying pan without fat. Cover and cook over a gentle fire for five to ten minutes, turning the pair, while still keeping them face to face, only once. The oil which emerges when they are heated is quite sufficient to cook them.

Finnan Haddock

Finnan haddock can simply be cooked under the grill and served with a little butter well rubbed into them, but perhaps the most attractive method is to poach them.

Pour a half-cup each of milk and water into a frying pan or fish pan so as to cover the fish. Cover and simmer for about fifteen minutes until tender, turning once, then transfer the fish to a hot plate and remove the skin and bones. Grind a little black pepper over them and dot with butter.

Finnan haddock is often served with a poached egg on top.

Bloaters

Bloaters are herring which are lightly cured while still fresh and without being preserved in salt. In the days when herring were still plentiful, the best bloaters came from Yarmouth, because the fish were in prime condition when the shoals arrived opposite the East Coast in October and November.

Like Arbroath Smokies, they should be eaten as soon as possible after curing — as André Simon remarks, 'To have them to perfection one must go to Yarmouth, and even there the epicure will eat them before he goes to bed rather than wait for breakfast.'

Kedgeree

Kedgeree is not a Scots dish, but takes its name from the Indian *Khitchri*, originally a dish of rice cooked with butter and a pea called *dál*. In its British version it may be made with a variety of cooked, flaked fish,

St Monace, one of the fishing villages of the East Neuk of Fife (Jan Read)

including Finnan haddock and salmon, or from canned tuna or ends of smoked salmon.

4 oz (110 g) rice	*Pepper and salt*
6 oz (170 g) butter	*Pinch turmeric or saffron powder*
1 shallot, chopped	*1 egg, hardboiled and chopped*
1 lb (450 g) fish, cooked	*Ground parsley*
and flaked	

Boil the rice in double its volume of water for about fifteen minutes until all the water has been absorbed and the grains are tender. Melt 2 oz (60 g) of butter in a frying pan and fry the chopped shallot until tender. Now stir in the rice, cooked fish and remainder of the butter, season with salt and pepper, then sprinkle in enough turmeric or saffron powder to tint the rice a light yellow, and lastly add the chopped, hardboiled egg. Pile on to a hot dish to serve, and garnish with parsley.

For those who like their kedgeree spiced, a little curry powder may be fried in the butter before addition of the rice.

Herrings in Oatmeal
A nourishing Scots dish and once a prime favourite for breakfast in country districts.

1 or 2 herring per person	*Oil for frying*
1 egg, beaten	*Ground parsley*
Salt and pepper	*Wedges of lemon*
Finely ground oatmeal for	
coating	

Ask the fishmonger to clean the fish (in Scotland it is already filleted when sold). Split down the side, open out flat and remove the backbone. Dip the fillets in beaten egg, season with salt and pepper, dredge in oatmeal and leave for thirty minutes so that the coating adheres firmly to the fish. Now heat a little oil in a frying pan and reduce the heat when it begins to smoke. Fry the fish slowly until golden-brown, remove surplus oil on kitchen paper, garnish with chopped parsley and serve very hot with wedges of lemon or with vinegar.

Fish Cakes
Grilled salmon or trout or fried fillets of fish (especially the small fillets of

haddock obtainable in Scotland) made an excellent breakfast, and the humble fish cake is by no means to be despised.

1 lb (450 g) soft white fish,
e.g. cod
Bouquet garni
½ lb (225 g) mashed potatoes
A little milk for mash
2 oz (60 g) butter

1 small onion, chopped fine
Yolk of 1 egg
Salt
Black pepper, freshly ground
Flour, a little for dusting

Simmer the fish with a *bouquet garni* for twenty minutes, then remove the skin and bones and pound it in a mortar. Boil the potatoes in salted water for twenty minutes and mash with a little milk and butter. Fry the chopped onion in butter, add to the mash and fish, together with the egg yolk, mix well and season. Now, with floured hands, shape the mixture into small cakes and fry in hot oil until golden.

Alternatively, dredge the cakes in the left-over, beaten white of egg and breadcrumbs before frying.

Pickled Herrings

Pickled herrings were a favourite breakfast dish from mediaeval times onwards — no doubt because salt herring was one of the few foodstuffs which could be preserved for use in winter. The recipe that follows is adapted from Mrs Dalgairns' *Practice of Cookery* of 1829. Salted herrings are still readily obtainable from fishmongers in Scotland.

6 salt herring
6 onions, thinly sliced
Salt and pepper

3 tablespoons brown sugar
Vinegar

Split the herring down the back and soak them overnight in cold water. In the morning, thoroughly rinse and clean them, remove the bones and cut them crosswise into strips ½-inch wide. Put the strips into a deep dish with the thinly sliced onions, sprinkle them with pepper and salt and the brown sugar, and cover them with vinegar. They will be ready for use in time for supper, and will keep for a week or more in a cool place.

CHAPTER V

Travellers' Fare

URING THE MIDDLE AGES few people travelled for pleasure;
such journeys as were undertaken on the primitive roads of the
time were for the more urgent reasons of business, war or state,
and common labourers were indeed forbidden to travel without a permit.
The only exceptions were pilgrimages to the shrine of a saint, and it was
in places such as Battle, Gloucester, Winchester and Canterbury that the
first inns were established to minister to the needs of the better-to-do
pilgrims. The nobility preferred to sojourn at monasteries or in the large
houses of their compeers, while the rest slept rough and sought refreshment at the country ale-houses, no more than cottages or huts distinguished by a pole carrying a few leafy branches. Even inns such as The
George at Glastonbury, which still survives, offered little more than
accommodation, and it was as well to arrive with one's own provender.

The first forms of public transport were the stage-wagons, introduced
about the middle of the sixteenth century and described by Thomas
Burke in his *Travel in England* as 'long, lumbering, springless, six-horsed
vehicles, which could take days on a journey from London to Winchester.' From this time onwards, and especially after the appearance of
the faster and more comfortable stage coaches between 1650 and 1660,
inns multiplied and their standards improved; but in Stuart times it
appears that travellers pressed on from breakfast until suppertime
without a pause for dinner, which was then about two o'clock.

Rather later, John Cresset, who wrote a pamphlet calling for the
suppression of stage coaches, made the bitter comment: 'What advantage
is it to men's health to be called out of their beds into their coaches an
hour before day in the morning... They are often brought to their inns
by torchlight, when it is too late to sit up to get a supper, and next

morning they are forced into the coach so early that they can get no breakfast....' It seems that, in addition to 'an old blunderbuss, a bag of bullets and a horn of gunpowder' for protection against highwaymen, the wise carried 'baskets of plum-cake, Dutch gingerbread, Cheshire cheese, Naples biscuits, macaroons, neat's tongues, and cold boiled beef; with bottles of usquebaugh [whisky], black-cherry brandy, cinnamon-water, sack [sherry], tent [Madeira], and strong beer.'

Of the hey-day of coach travel, between 1800 and the advent of the railways in the 1830's, Thomas Burke reports that, 'What had been gained by better appointments, better springs, and better everything else, was lost by rush and hurry. The coaches, mail and stage, stopped at appointed places for breakfast and dinner, but their time-tables worked so much to the minute that the stop scarcely gave the passengers time to get anything like a meal. Ten minutes was allowed for breakfast, and for dinner twenty minutes.... Sometimes unscrupulous innkeepers bribed the drivers and guard to get the company out, with their "Time's up,

Nineteenth-century travellers summoned from breakfast; above them hang the hams in their outdoor safe (contemporary print)

gentlemen — can't wait — must go!'' some minutes short of the twenty minutes; or ordered waiters to put the joints in front of the ladies because they were slow carvers.'

A rosier picture of a coach breakfast is that of Thomas Hughes: 'The table was covered with the whitest of white cloths and of china, and bore a pigeon-pie, a ham, a round of cold beef; and a waiter came in with a tray of kidneys, and steaks, and eggs and bacon, and toast and muffins, and coffee and tea.'

The German princeling, Pückler Muskau, who visited England in 1826, complained of the high cost of posting, but found the inns 'neat and well-attended' and has this to say of their breakfasts:

Englishmen who do not belong to the aristocracy, and are not very rich, usually travel without a servant by the mail or stage coach, which deposits them at the inn. The man who waits on strangers to the coach, cleans their boots, etc., has the universal appellation of Boots. It is, accordingly, Boots who brings you your slippers, helps you to pull off your boots, and then departs, first asking at what time you will have, not, as in Germany, coffee, but your hot water to shave. He appears with it punctually at the appointed hour, and brings your clothes, cleanly brushed. The Traveller then hastens to dress himself and to return to his beloved coffee room, where the ingredients of breakfast are richly spread upon the table. To this meal he seems to bring more animation than to any other, and, indeed, I think more appetite; for the number of cups of tea, the masses of bread and butter, eggs and cold meat which he devours awaken silent envy in the breast, or rather in the stomach of the less capable foreigner. He is not only permitted, but enjoined (by custom, his gospel) to read. At every cup of tea he unfolds a newspaper of the size of a table-cloth. Not a single speech, crim. con., murder or other catastrophe, invented by the accident-maker in London escapes him.

Like one who would rather die of a surfeit than leave anything uneaten which he has paid for, the systematic Englishman thinks that, having called for a newspaper, he ought not to leave a letter of it unread. By this means his breakfast lasts several hours, and the sixth or seventh cup is drunk cold. I have seen this glorious meal protracted so long that it is blended with dinner; and you will hardly believe me when I assure you that a light supper followed at midnight without the company quitting the table.

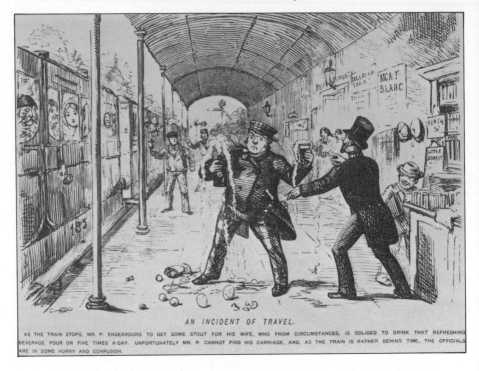

AN INCIDENT OF TRAVEL.

AS THE TRAIN STOPS, MR. P. ENDEAVOURS TO GET SOME STOUT FOR HIS WIFE, WHO FROM CIRCUMSTANCES, IS OBLIGED TO DRINK THAT REFRESHING BEVERAGE FOUR OR FIVE TIMES A-DAY. UNFORTUNATELY MR. P. CANNOT FIND HIS CARRIAGE, AND, AS THE TRAIN IS RATHER BEHIND TIME, THE OFFICIALS ARE IN SOME HURRY AND CONFUSION.

'An Incident of Travel' (cartoon by Leech from Punch, *1856)*

Within a decade of the opening in 1830 of the Liverpool and Manchester Railway, which, in its first year, carried more than 445,000 passengers — despite the discomfort of wooden seats in the second class and open trucks for the third — the mail coaches had been taken off the road, most of the stage coaches had been withdrawn and formerly populous inns were closing all over the country.

Until the 1870's there were no corridor coaches on the trains, and passengers on the trunk routes from London to Scotland, Wales and the South West often faced journeys of eight to ten hours without toilets or catering facilities. Certain stations were therefore designated as refreshment stops; but all the old complaints about rushed meals at coaching inns at once resurfaced in new form. Wolverton was notorious for its scalding coffee, and when the unfortunate traveller asked for milk to cool it, it was served on the boil.

'At another station,' as Thomas Burke reports, 'where the usual five-minute stop for refreshments was made, the writer was one of many who had just secured a cup of coffee, when the bell rang, and the call came: "Take your seats, please!" They left their coffee, and dashed to the train, and the train stood for another three minutes. Before it left, they saw their full cups of coffee emptied back in the urn for the next train.'

Of particularly ill-repute was the refreshment room at Swindon, where all the trains from London to the South-West or to South Wales stopped for ten minutes. In its early days the Great Western had conceded a lease to an outside caterer, and long after other railway companies were operating restaurant cars, unfortunate train-loads of passengers *en route* from Paddington to Penzance, with a further seven-and-a-half hour journey in prospect, were disgorged on to the platform to battle for a drink and snack to take back to their compartments.

One of the most vociferous of critics was Charles Dickens:

What with skimming over the open landscape, what with mining in the damp bowels of the earth, what with banging, booming, and shrieking the scores of miles away, I am hungry when I arrive at the 'refreshment' station where I am expected. Please to observe — expected.... The apartment that is to restore me is a wind-trap

The scramble in a Victorian station buffet – at York (Illustrated London News, *1892*)

During the early 1930s the Great Western Railway was still selling breakfast baskets at main stations

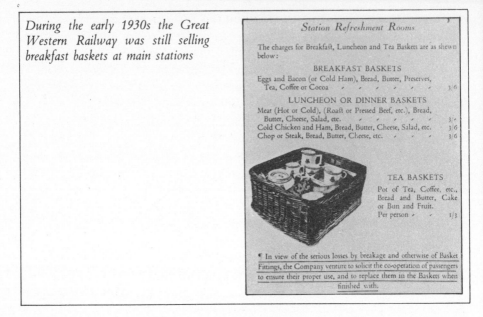

Station Refreshment Rooms

The charges for Breakfast, Luncheon and Tea Baskets are as shewn below:

BREAKFAST BASKETS

Eggs and Bacon (or Cold Ham), Bread, Butter, Preserves, Tea, Coffee or Cocoa 3/6

LUNCHEON OR DINNER BASKETS

Meat (Hot or Cold), (Roast or Pressed Beef, etc.), Bread, Butter, Cheese, Salad, etc. 3/-
Cold Chicken and Ham, Bread, Butter, Cheese, Salad, etc. 3/6
Chop or Steak, Bread, Butter, Cheese, etc. 3/6

TEA BASKETS

Pot of Tea, Coffee, etc., Bread and Butter, Cake or Bun and Fruit.
Per person 1/3

¶ In view of the serious losses by breakage and otherwise of Basket Fittings, the Company venture to solicit the co-operation of passengers to ensure their proper use, and to replace them in the Baskets when finished with.

cunningly set to inveigle all the draughts in the countryside, and to communicate a special intensity to them as they rotate in two hurricanes; one about my wretched head, one about my wretched legs. The training of the young ladies behind the counter has been directed on the assumption of a defiant dramatic show that I am *not* expected... Chilling fast, and subdued by the moral disadvantage at which I stand, I turn my disconsolate eyes on the refreshments that are to restore me. I find that I must either scald my throat by insanely ladling into it, against time and for no wager, brown hot water stiffened with flour; or I must make myself flaky and sick with Banbury cake; or I must stuff into my delicate organisation a currant pin-cushion which I know will swell.

One solution was to purchase a breakfast at the station of departure, which, for 3/6d, might contain eggs and bacon (or cold ham), bread, butter, preserves, tea, coffee or cocoa. The resourceful Major L... observes of the fare at railway stations that 'necessarily it depends on the consumption whether the sandwiches are freshly cut, the chicken freshly roasted, and *in summer* both are liable to be sprinkled with dust, a sauce which, so far as the Author is a judge, improves neither the taste nor digestion.' He therefore '*strongly* advises every one who prefers a nice clean luncheon to take their own.'

Dickens was also scathing in his comments on the railway hotels, which, as the nineteenth century wore on, took the place of the old coaching inns. So, he talks of new walls with the gritty feeling of mortar, cracked doors and warped shutters, and furniture which was always in the wrong place. As to the ubiquitous mortar, it blocked the bedroom chimneys and even pervaded the sandwiches and sherry, while the clientele was as green and impersonal as the establishments generally.

His remarks sort oddly today, when the railway hotels stand four-square, monuments to the solid comforts and affluence of the Victorian era. The first, at Euston, opened in 1839, was built in two parts, a superior establishment for first-class passengers, managed by the aptly-named Mr Bacon, a former steward of the Athenaeum, and the unpretentious Victoria, intended for overnight guests and officially described as a 'dormitory and coffee room'.

The private railway companies were later to vie with one another in the splendour of their hotels: the 700-bedroom Grand Central boasted a

One of the great railway hotels, the Midland in Manchester

The Refreshment Room at Manchester Exchange Station, June 1885

cycle-track on the roof (for guests to work off the heavy meals?); at York there was a printing shop to produce the elaborate menus and wine lists and also, once restaurant cars had been introduced, to rush off changes in the menu while the train waited in the station; but plushiest of all was Sir George Gilbert Scott's Gothic palace at St Pancras, equipped with gasoliers, electric bells, dust chutes, hydraulic lifts, a rubber-surfaced cab-rank to deaden the noise, telephones to listen in to performances at theatres and concert halls, and a Moorish alcove on the stairs dispensing Turkish coffee. In its day, it was described as 'the most sumptuous and best-conducted hotel in the Empire'.

The breakfasts served in these temples of Victorian tycoons from the burgeoning Midlands and North were in scale with their all-embracing opulence. One is still assured of a decent breakfast in the British Transport Hotels, where there is no nonsense, as at some 'luxury hotels', about extricating prepacked croissants from a mini-bar in the bedroom and making one's own coffee.

The first full meal to be served on a British train was in 1874, when the Midland Railway introduced Pullman cars in the American style, staged a run from St Pancras to Bedford and offered lunch to the assembled press. However, it was not until November 1879, on the service between Leeds and King's Cross, that the Great Northern Railway fitted out another Pullman car, the *Prince of Wales*, as a regular dining car in which lunch or dinner was prepared and cooked *en route*. In 1891, when trains with through corridors were in general service, the Great Eastern Railway introduced a three-coach dining set on its Harwich boat train, where breakfasts and other hot meals were for the first time available to third-class passengers.

During the early Edwardian period no expense was spared to make dining cars as similar as possible to a luxurious restaurant. In the words of Geoffrey Kichenside's *The Restaurant Car*, 'Damasks were used for curtains or blinds, seats were covered in leather, attractive floral printed material, or velvet; walnut, satinwood or other timbers were used for interior panelling, some of which was often skilfully figured or inlaid.' And it became possible to breakfast in the most surprising circumstances. In 1910 the Metropolitan Railway inaugurated a Pullman service on its rush-hour trains, enabling the harrassed businessman both to breakfast or take afternoon tea on his way in or out of the City.

The price of a three-course breakfast, including both kippers or fried fish followed by bacon and eggs or a grill, with the usual toast and marmalade, was still only 3/6d up to and during the first year or two of the Second World War, when I [J. R.] remember dealing with just such a repast on a train lost in a world of its own, as the snow came down over the Forth Bridge.

There is, indeed, a mystique about the breed of railway waiters and the British restaurant car, of which Paul Jennings, writing in the *Observer* in 1962, noted that 'we had more ... than France, Belgium, Italy, Spain, Western Germany, Scandinavia, the Netherlands and Luxembourg put together.' He continues:

... *Our* restaurant cars nurse the inner life of our railway shires, where lonely George Eliot farmhouses stand in tufted meadows and small roads curve away round low green hills. Never mind about London-Birmingham; there is a restaurant car on a train that every day makes the unimaginable journey from Ipswich to Liverpool. And if a train doesn't have a full restaurant car ... the time-table says RB — buffet

The Prince of Wales, the first restaurant car in service with a British railway, the Great Northern (Illustrated London News, *November 1879*)

The smoking saloon and kitchen of the Prince of Wales, an adapted Pullman car (Illustrated London News, *1879*)

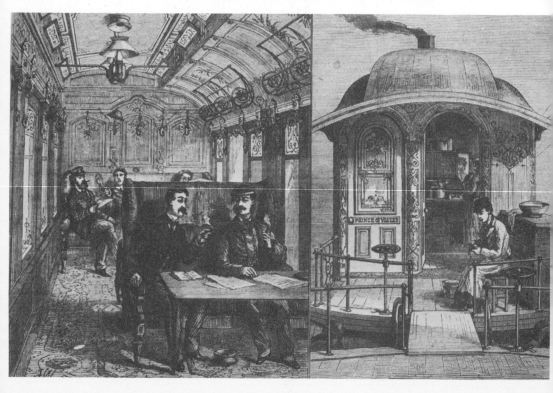

car, or the even smaller MB — miniature buffet, just one man serving from a little kind of pantry. Doubtless on very minor routes there are even smaller subdivisions, tiny waiters going around with little boxes containing mouse sandwiches, noggins of soup, thimbles of lemonade....

Happily, it is still possible to obtain a Great British Breakfast on British Rail's Inter-City Trains — though no longer, alas, for 3/6d. After the usual preliminaries, including fruit juice, cereal or porridge, the menu lists:

THE GRILL TRAY

2 Rashers of Back Bacon, 2 Sausages, Fried Egg,
Mushrooms, Tomato, Sauté Potatoes and Fried Bread

or

FISH DISH

Grilled Kippers
Poached Haddock "Arnold Bennet" — [smoked haddock
poached in milk and topped with a poached egg]

Toast, Croissants, French Toast, Bread Rolls, Crispbread,
Selection of Marmalades including Frank Cooper's Oxford

BTH own-blend Coffee
Pot of freshly brewed Tea

Before taking leave of the railway breakfast, it seems in order to mention the achievement of Norman D. MacDonald, one of a small band of enthusiasts who travelled, stop-watches in hand, at the height of the railway races to Aberdeen, on the East Coast Flier on the night of April 19, 1895. It is recorded *verbatim* by O. S. Nock in *Railway Race to the North*:

I did the feat of having four breakfasts in four divers places. (1) Soon after midnight one of my co-lunatics in our "sleeper" produced a flask and very massive sandwiches. (2) After Berwick-on-Tweed the attendant gave us coffee and biscuits. (3) Not long after 5 a.m. we were

Refreshment Trolley, Derby Station, February 1908

hammering on the doors of the Imperial Hotel in Aberdeen calling for food. On getting in I said the Cockney pressmen must have real porridge for once, "and mind they have milk, all proper, and no beastly treacle or sugar." The poor waiter said, "There is no milk!" I blazed into Highland fire, which he damped down by saying, "Man! the coos is no milket yet!" (4) I caught the "Flying Scotsman" portion from Aberdeen and landed in Edinburgh at 9.40 a.m., dashed to my nearby house to find the joyful remains of the family feed still on the table. I had done nearly 200 miles between my second and third breakfasts and about 130 miles between the third and fourth ones!

Wherever the British have travelled, worked and settled, as far as the outposts of Empire, they have insisted on their substantial cooked breakfast. Since the symbol and lifeline of Empire were the ships plying the oceans of the world, it is hardly surprising that in them too the tradition flourished. With the introduction of refrigeration and cold stores in the latter years of the nineteenth century and with their extensive galleys, ships were in fact better-placed to mount a really comprehensive breakfast than the trains with their cramped kitchens. And, after all, with nothing more in prospect than a game of deck quoits or a good book with a mid-morning cup of beef tea in a sheltered deckchair, what better place to do justice to it?

For decades the P & O, or Peninsular and Oriental Steam Navigation Company, to give it its full name, ferried soldiers, administrators, merchants, globe-trotters and their families to India and places east, absorbing its main competitors, the British India and Orient Lines. It was famous for its breakfasts; but perhaps the most elaborate were served on the transatlantic services to North America by Cunard-White Star and its foreign rivals. In the days between the World Wars, when Cunard, the French Line, The Italian Line, the United States Line and Nord-deutscher Lloyd fought for the Blue Riband of the Atlantic, gastronomy was as important as a turn of speed.

Conoisseurs consider that the *Normandie* had the edge over the other great liners for the elegance and inventiveness of her cuisine, but certainly Cunard yielded to no one in the scope of its breakfasts, a compendium of all that one might expect in a large country house of the preceding period — as is evident from the menu of the R.M.S. *Lancastria* for October 3, 1935, reproduced on the jacket. In a somewhat splendid gesture, with the choice at breakfast running to hundreds of items, the Italians retaliated by issuing no menu to first-class passengers, but advising them that anything which they wished to order was available on request.

Second and third-class passengers breakfasted and dined separately, and the menus were more restricted, though still more than ample. A sodden menu retrieved from the pocket of one of the unfortunate passengers drowned in the *Titanic* disaster of 1912 records that the third-class breakfast served on the morning before included porridge, tripe and onions and potatoes baked in their jackets! In the hey-day of the liners, children even had their own menus.

I [J. R.] must confess that, as a child, I was myself interested in heartier fare. As a small boy of five, I can remember returning from Sydney to England in the *Demosthenes*, belonging to the old Aberdeen Line. During a voyage of some eight weeks via the Cape of Good Hope, the ship ran into a storm in the Australian Bight; and leaving my parents prostrate in their cabin, I accompanied my even smaller brother to an entirely deserted and heaving dining salon, where we ordered — and duly consumed — large platters of mutton collops, with no ill effects at all. On the *Demosthenes*, I struck up a lively friendship with our cabin steward, lending him my cherished copy of *The Wonder Book of Ships*. Having spent my first five years in a semi-tropical country, I had never seen snow or ice, and it was he who conducted me to the ship's cold store, with the hams and sides of beef hanging in serried ranks, where I made my first snowball!

Apart from cruise ships, such as the *Q. E. II*, which in some way carry on the old tradition, ocean-going liners are now a nostalgic memory. One wonders what Charles Dickens and the others, who lamented the passing of the stage coaches and posting inns, would have had to say of the rubbery ham salad and tired roll, plastic-packed by a caterer in some anonymous airport, which do duty for breakfast in the economy class of today's airlines.

OATMEAL AND POTATOES

OATMEAL

Porridge

Porridge may, of course, be made very rapidly with proprietary 'Porridge Oats', following the directions on the packet — but this is not the method of the self-respecting Scot. F. Marian McNeill, who was a perfectionist, recommends the use of fresh spring water and Midlothian oats, 'unsurpassed the world over'. According to her, the One and Only Method is as follows:

'Bring the water to the boil and as soon as it reaches boiling point add the oatmeal, letting it fall in a steady rain from the left hand and stirring it briskly the while with the right . . . . Be careful to avoid lumps, unless the children clamour for them. When the porridge is boiling steadily, draw the mixture to the side and put on the lid. Let it cook from twenty to thirty minutes according to the quality of the oatmeal, and do not add the salt, which has a tendency to harden the meal and prevent its swelling, until it has cooked for at least ten minutes. On the other hand, never cook porridge without salt. Ladle straight into porringers or soup plates and serve with small individual bowls of cream, or milk, or buttermilk. Each spoonful of porridge, which should be very hot, is dipped in the cream or milk, which should be quite cold, before it is conveyed to the mouth.'

She adds: 'Children often like a layer of sugar, honey, syrup or treacle, or of raw oatmeal on top. A morsel of butter in the centre of the plate agrees with some digestions better than milk.'

Aigar Brose

Aigar (or Oatmeal) Brose and Gruel were at one time favourite and nourishing alternatives to porridge in Scotland. Brose is made very simply by putting a handful or two of oatmeal into a bowl with a knob of butter and a little salt, and adding boiling water to cover. Stir vigorously until it forms knots and serve with 'sour dook' (buttermilk) or ordinary milk.

Oatcakes

Oatcakes go very well with marmalade and honey instead of toast; in Scotland they serve both.

4 oz (110 g) medium oatmeal	*1 level tablespoon bacon fat*
Pinch of bicarbonate of soda	*or dripping*
¾ teaspoon salt	*Boiling water*

Mix the oatmeal with the bicarbonate and the salt, then melt the fat with a tablespoon of water and pour into a well in the middle. Flour a baking board, knead thoroughly and roll out as thinly as possible, sprinkling both sides with dry meal to avoid sticking. Cut into triangles, place on a floured baking sheet and bake in a moderately hot oven (400° F, 200° C, Mark 6) for about twenty to thirty minutes until the cakes are crisp and the edges begin to curl up. The oatcakes may alternatively be cooked on a hot griddle on top of the stove until the edges curl and then lightly toasted in the oven.

POTATOES

Sauté Potatoes

In Scotland, a few sauté potatoes are often served with eggs and bacon.

Peel and parboil (but do not over-boil) the potatoes for about ten minutes according to size. Remove and cut into thin slices. Heat a little fat or cooking oil in a frying pan until short of smoking, add the potatoes and shake the pan. When cooked on one side, turn the slices and brown the other. Remove with a slotted spoon and toss on kitchen paper to absorb excess fat. Serve at once.

Potato Cakes

Another adjunct to bacon and eggs, popular with the thrifty Scots housewife. They are made very simply by shaping left-over mashed

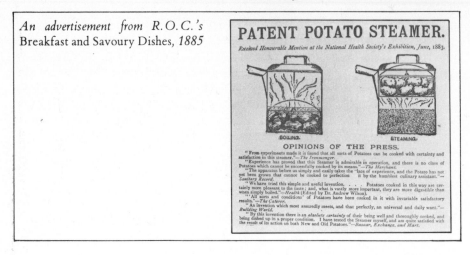

An advertisement from R.O.C.'s Breakfast and Savoury Dishes, *1885*

PATENT POTATO STEAMER.

Received Honourable Mention at the National Health Society's Exhibition, June, 1883.

BOILING.   STEAMING.

OPINIONS OF THE PRESS.

" From experiments made it is found that all sorts of Potatoes can be cooked with certainty and satisfaction in this steamer."—*The Ironmonger.*

" Experience has proved that this Steamer is admirable in operation, and there is no class of Potatoes which cannot be successfully cooked by its means."—*The Merchant.*

" The apparatus before us simply and easily takes the "face of experience, and the Potato has not yet been grown that cannot be cooked to perfection it by the humblest culinary assistant."—*Sanitary Record.*

" We have tried this simple and useful invention. . . . Potatoes cooked in this way are certainly more pleasant to the taste ; and, what is vastly more important, they are more digestible than when simply boiled."—*Health* (Edited by Dr. Andrew Wilson).

" All sorts and conditions' of Potatoes have been cooked in it with invariable satisfactory results."—*The Caterer.*

" An invention which most assuredly meets, and that perfectly, an universal and daily want."—*Building World.*

" By this invention there is an *absolute certainty* of their being well and thoroughly cooked, and being dished up in a proper condition. I have tested the Steamer myself, and am quite satisfied with the result of its action on both New and Old Potatoes.—*Bazaar, Exchange, and Mart.*

potato into a thin cake, coating with a little flour and frying on both sides in hot fat or cooking oil.

Potato Scones

This Scots speciality resembles a thin pancake more than a scone. They may be buttered, fresh from the girdle and hot, and eaten on the side ; but are also fried and served with grilled bacon or bacon and eggs.

1 lb (450 g) potatoes, peeled	*1 oz (30 g) butter or margarine*
1 teaspoon salt	*3-4 oz (80-110 g) flour*

Boil, drain and sieve the potatoes. Add the salt and butter and knead into a stiff dough with as much flour as it will absorb. Roll out to about 1/4-inch thick on a floured board, cut into triangles and prick with a fork. Bake on a hot greased griddle for about five minutes each side until browned.

CHAPTER VI

Home Thoughts from Abroad

A T ITS BEST the Continental Breakfast bears little resemblance to what passes as such today in too many English hotels, where, for lack of staff or simply because the management is lazy, one is faced with a few tired buns, half-liquid butter clinging to its foil wrapper and a cup of instant coffee. One thinks nostalgically of French provincial hotels with their drab carpets and brass bedsteads and of trays, served in the room or on a balcony dappled by lime trees, and piled with light, flaky *croissants*, crusty bread fresh from the baker, firm white country butter, jars of honey and huge cups of *café au lait*, bitter with the taste of chicory.

In Spain, too, one breakfasted well on *churros* — fluted, golden-brown fingers, smoking from the olive oil in which they are fried like doughnuts, but lighter and less stodgy and sweet, washed down with a cup of chocolate so thick that the spoon stands upright in it.

Across the Channel things are not always what they were. During a recent visit to Catalonia, and with the excuse that the kitchen staff did not put in an appearance until 9.30 and that fresh bread was not delivered until later, we were served with an entire breakfast encased in Cellophane — 'Bimbo' (a proprietary toast in the form of a rusk), *magdalenas* (sweet cakes, which settle in the tummy like lead), sticky butter in foil and foil-topped containers of a saccharine apricot compôte. Having marked the packets and so checked that the identical *magdalenas* reappeared each morning, we hit on a way of shaming the proprietors into providing something better. This was to ring for *café completo*, smartly to leave the room for the baker's shop on the corner, and to return with a couple of unwrapped bars of fresh bread, purposely flourishing them outside the reception desk on the way back.

But however appetizing the Continental Breakfast, it is difficult to supplement it with more than *oeufs à la coque*, and the Briton abroad yearns for more substantial fare. If Sir Walter Scott is to be believed — and he is a reliable guide — the Scots who served in France at the time of the Auld Alliance did not suffer from short commons, and it was with no *petit déjeuner* that Maitre Pierre entertained Quentin Durward:

> The breakfast... was admirable. There was a *Pâté de Perigord*, over which a gastronome would have wished to live and die, like Homer's lotus-eaters, forgetful of kin, native country, and all social obligations whatever... There was a decent *ragoût*, with just that *petit point de l'ail* which Gascons love and Scottishmen do not hate. There was, besides, a delicate ham, which had once supported a noble wild boar in the neighbouring wood of Montrichard. There was the most exquisite white bread, made into little round loaves called *boules* (whence the bakers took their French name of *boulangers*) of which the crust was so inviting that, even with water alone, it would have been a delicacy. But the water was not alone, for there was a flask of leather called *boittrine*, which contained almost a quart of exquisite *vin de Beaulne*...
>
> "The best meal I have eaten," said the youth, "since I left Glen-houlakin"....
>
> "The Scottish Archers of the Guard eat as good a one or better every day," his host assured him.

Something of the same pathos comes through, centuries later, in Somerset Maugham's *Three Fat Women of Antibes*, when Frank [Frances] Hickson discovered that one of her companions had abandoned her regimen:

> "Beatrice, what are you doing?" she cried in her deep voice. It was like the roll of thunder in the distant mountains.
>
> Beatrice looked at her coolly.
>
> "Eating," she answered.
>
> "Damn it, I can see you're eating."
>
> In front of Beatrice was a plate of *croissants* and a plate of butter, a pot of strawberry jam, coffee and a jug of cream. Beatrice was spreading butter thick on delicious hot bread, covering this with jam, and then pouring the thick cream over all.
>
> "You'll kill yourself," said Frank.
>
> "I don't care," mumbled Beatrice with her mouth full.
>
> "You'll put on pounds and pounds."
>
> "Go to hell!"

The Auction Mart Coffee Room, London, c. 1810

The kitchen at Christ Church, after A. Pugin, 1813

Eggcups from the historical collection of Mrs Anne O'Shea

'Breakfast at Bourgueil' (contemporary eighteenth-century print)

She actually laughed in Frank's face. My God, how good those *croissants* smelt . . . !

The tears welled up to Frank's eyes. Suddenly she felt very weak and womanly . . . Speechless she sank down on to a chair by Beatrice's side. A waiter came up. With a pathetic gesture she waved towards the coffee and the *croissants*.

"I'll have the same," she sighed.

That, during the period of the Grand Tour and throughout the nineteenth century, the British asked for and expected to get their normal breakfasts on the Continent is evident from the 'new and carefully revised' 1874 edition of *A Handbook of Travel-Talk*, printed in question-and-answer form in four languages: English, German, French and Italian. The battered volume in front of me [J.R.], with its worn red-cloth binding and yellowing pages, was actually used by my father during his student days in Zürich.

The *Handbook* first deals with the contingencies of the Traveller ('T') on his journey:

T. The horses run against the post — the bridge — the tree
T. The carriage is near the precipice
T. One of the wheels is off
T. The axle-tree is broken
T. The coachman (postilion) is drunk — impertinent — foolhardy . . .
T. Oh, dear! The postilion has been thrown (off) down . . .
T. It rains in torrents
T. It lightens — it thunders
T. Can the horses not wade through?
    No, Sir; the rush of the waters is too violent
T. I am really much alarmed

Even the trains were not entirely safe, hence the Traveller's ejaculation to the guard: 'We are dreadfully shaken up in this carriage; I think it is not screwed up sufficiently.' Arrival, too, posed its problems:

T. I want you to carry our luggage as far as the summit of the pass — to the other side of the pass — over the glacier.

After this, it is hardly surprising that he stood in need of solid sustenance:

    What do you wish to eat?
T. I wish a meat breakfast.
    What will you take along with your tea, coffee — chops, beef-steak?
T. I should like a little cold meat — a mutton chop — beefsteak — a slice of ham — fresh eggs.
    Do you prefer rolls — or household bread — or brown bread — or stale bread?
T. I should like plain tea, two cups, with some bread and butter. I want some honey — some preserves. Make some toast. Give us some fresh eggs, but do not boil them more than three minutes.

And their exchanges end on a sour note:

T. These eggs are not boiled enough. They are not fresh. Give me some new bread. The coffee is not strong. It is too weak . . . Take it away (*Nehmen Sie weg – Emportez-les – Portàtele via*).

Insistence on a good breakfast remains one of the most typical traits of the British exile abroad, so *Vogue* of November 5, 1968, prefacing its report with the scathing comment that 'even the most beauty-conscious women' blithely ignore that 'instinctive grasp of the rules that govern health and well-being' and 'rush out of the house with a cup of black coffee, or nothing at all aboard', while their more sensible husbands 'eat a jolly good breakfast', proceeds to an account of the breakfasts enjoyed by the late Duke of Windsor during his sojourn in Paris.

It seems that the Duke was particularly partial to scrambled eggs with creamed haddock; kedgeree of turbot, salmon, haddock, or other fish, with mango chutney and curry sauce; chicken hash with bacon; eggs fried with cream; bacon and *croissants*; scones and muffins, and always 'some kind of bread or toast and orange marmalade'.

The *Handbook of Travel-Talk* gives one some idea of the insular and imperious attitude of the British abroad, paralleled, one is tempted to think, by that of their American cousins at a later period; but for a blow-by-blow account of culinary adventures on the Continent one must return to the inimitable Mr Jorrocks.

'Jorrocks's France, in three wolumes, would sound werry well,' observed our worthy citizen, one afternoon, to his confidential companion the Yorkshireman, as they sat in the veranda in Coram Street, eating red currants and supping cold whiskey punch.

A week later they were boarding the superb paddle-steamer *Royal George* at Dover.

Who shall describe the misery that ensued? The groans and moans of the sufferers, increasing every moment, as the vessel heaved and dived, and rolled and creaked, while hand-basins multiplied as half-sick passengers caught the green countenance and fixed eye of some prostrate sufferer and were overcome themselves.

Mr Jorrocks, what with his Margate trips, and a most substantial breakfast of beef-steaks and porter, tea, eggs, muffins, prawns and fried ham, held out as long as anybody — indeed, at one time the odds were that he would not be sick at all . . . .

But it was not to be. After an acrimonious encounter with his acquaintance Sergeant Bumptious, who broke off their conversation by giving 'a

'A Margate Packet – The Effects of a Squall or a Sudden Shift of Ballast', 1821

donation to the fishes', Jorrocks observed 'with apparent mildness and compassion, "Now, my dear sergeant, to show you that I can return good for evil, allow me to fatch you a nice 'ot mutton chop! . . . Or perhaps you'd prefer a cut of boiled beef with yellow fat and a dab of cabbage?" an alternative which was too powerful for the worthy citizen himself — for, like Sterne with his captive, he had drawn a picture that his own imagination could not sustain — and in attempting to reach the side of the boat, he cascaded over the sergeant, and they rolled over each other, senseless and helpless on the deck.'

Restored to *terra firma*, Mr Jorrocks took coach for Paris along a road on which the innkeepers were evidently alive to the needs of their British clientele, for 'They breakfasted at Beaumont, and had a regular spread of fish, beef-steak, mutton chops, a large joint of hot roast veal, roast chickens, several yards of sour bread, grapes, peaches, pears and plums, with vin ordinaire, and coffee au lait.' Jorrocks was, unfortunately, still 'off his feed, and stood all the time to ease his haunches.'

On their arrival in Paris, problems of provender and accommodation immediately arose; but Mr Jorrocks had in the meantime shared a seat in the coach with a French lady, "approaching to middle age, with a nice smart plump figure, good hazel-coloured eyes, a beautiful foot and ankle, and very well dressed. Indeed her dress very materially reduced the appearance of her age, and she was what the milliners would call remarkably well "got up".' An enquiry from her negro serving-boy, Agamemnon, elicited that she was none other than "Madame la Countess Benwolio, a werry grande femme", and Jorrocks's problem was solved when she suggested that he moved into her 'splendid house in the Rue des Mauvais-Garçons, ornamented with mirrors, musical clocks, and he didn't know what.'

"You shall manger cinque fois every day," said she. "Cinque fois," she repeated. "Humph!" said Mr Jorrocks to himself, "what can that mean? — cank four — four times five's twenty — eat twenty times a day — not possible!" "Oui, Monsieur, cinque fois," repeated the Countess, telling the number off on her fingers — "Café at nine of the matin, déjeuner à la fourchette at onze o'clock, dinner at cinque heures, café at six hour, and souper at neuf hour." "Upon my word," replied Mr Jorrocks, his eyes sparkling with pleasure, "your offer is werry inviting...."

Inviting, but as it turned out, very expensive; for after Jorrocks had munched his way through innumerable breakfasts and other meals, including a dinner at the Café de Paris, beginning with oysters and progressing through *entrée de boeuf*, quail, snipe, artichokes *à la sauce blanche, Charlotte de pommes* ('the crust is browned to a turn, and the rich apricot sweetmeat lies ensconsed in the middle, like a sleeping babe in its cradle'), followed by Roquefort, Gruyère and Neufchatel, and washed down with Chablis, Champagne, St Julien and 'claret of light Hermitage', he was ejected from his lodgings on the appearance of a better-paying client, 'a monstrous Dutchman with a green patch on his right eye'. The 'Countess' was implacable and after presenting Jorrocks with a bill 'reaching down each side of his body and round his waist', ordered Agamemnon to bundle his clothes into his portmanteau.

Overcharging was, of course, the continual complaint of Victorian travellers on the Continent, hence the pregnant phrase in the section entitled 'Paying the Bill' in the *Handbook of Travel-Talk*: 'T. What! So much. That is impossible.'

But if today's Innocent Abroad feels that he has paid over the odds for his cooked breakfast, let him reflect on the plight of a Mr Bernard Keefe, who recently wrote to the *Guardian* to report that, after paying £46 for a double room with breakfast in a Bath hotel, he was later charged £1.70 for coffee and £5.60 for scrambled eggs.

BREADS AND TOAST

Bread has, of course, always been a staple of the breakfast table. The pity is that so much of the sliced, packaged bread sold today is bland and tasteless. Things are better in Scotland, where fresh, crusty loaves are still made by small firms in the traditional ovens — perhaps because, as F. Marian McNeill suggests, 'Scottish professional bakers learnt the art from France centuries ago, whereas few English bakers made bread equal to what Englishwomen made at home.'

Breadmaking is beyond the scope of this book, and readers who wish to make their own are referred to Elizabeth David's comprehensive book on the subject* or the useful little *Home Baked* by George and Cecilia Scurfield; but here is F. Marian McNeill's recipe from the *Book of Breakfasts* for Scots Morning Rolls or Baps:

Morning Rolls

1 lb (450 g) flour	1 oz (30 g) baker's yeast
Salt	Sugar
2 oz (60 g) lard	¼ pint (150 ml) milk

Sift a pound of flour into a warm bowl and mix with it a small teaspoonful of salt. Rub in, with the finger-tips, two ounces of lard. In another bowl cream an ounce of yeast and a teaspoonful of sugar (that is work them together with a wooden spoon till liquid); add ½-pint of tepid milk and water (half and half), and strain into the flour. Make a soft dough, cover, and set to rise for an hour in a warm place. Knead lightly and divide into pieces of equal size to form oval shapes about three inches long and two wide. Brush with milk or water (to give a glaze) and, if 'floury baps' are desired, dust them with flour just after brushing them, and again just before they go into the oven. Place the baps on a greased and floured tin and set again in a warm place, to prove, for fifteen minutes. To prevent blisters, press a finger in the centre of each before they are placed in the oven. Bake in a hot oven from fifteen to twenty minutes. Baps

* *English Bread and Yeast Cooking.* Allen Lane, 1977

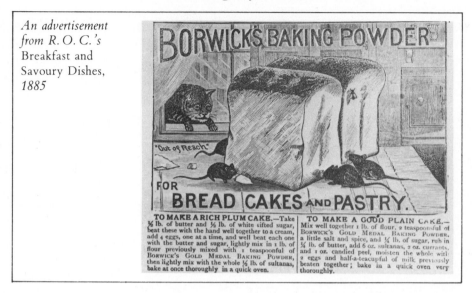

An advertisement from R. O. C.'s Breakfast and Savoury Dishes, 1885

BORWICK'S BAKING POWDER

"Out of Reach"

FOR BREAD CAKES AND PASTRY.

TO MAKE A RICH PLUM CAKE.—Take ½ lb. of butter and ½ lb. of white sifted sugar, beat these with the hand well together to a cream, add 4 eggs, one at a time, and well beat each one with the butter and sugar, lightly mix in 1 lb. of flour previously mixed with 1 teaspoonful of BORWICK'S GOLD MEDAL BAKING POWDER, then lightly mix with the whole ½ lb. of sultanas, bake at once thoroughly in a quick oven.

TO MAKE A GOOD PLAIN CAKE.— Mix well together 1 lb. of flour, 2 teaspoonsful of BORWICK'S GOLD MEDAL BAKING POWDER, a little salt and spice, and ¼ lb. of sugar, rub in ¼ lb. of butter, add 6 oz. sultanas, 2 oz. currants, and 1 oz. candied peel, moisten the whole with 2 eggs and half-a-teacupful of milk previously beaten together; bake in a quick oven very thoroughly.

appear exclusively on the breakfast-table, and should be eaten warm from the oven.

Toast
Toast is of two kinds, thin and brittle as sometimes served at dinner, or the thick toast, brown and crisp on the outside and spongy in the middle, as usually eaten at breakfast.

Thick toast is at its most appetizing when made with a toasting fork in front of a hot, glowing fire, when it has a lightness and smoky flavour all of its own — but for most of us this is now only a childhood memory. The principle is the same when making it under a grill. Fresh bread, not more than a day old, should be cut into slices about ¼.inch thick, and the grill must be really hot. Toast placed very near the grill and done quickly will be almost charred on the outside and spongy in the middle, while if placed too far away and done very slowly, it will be firm all through. One should aim at a compromise, and, of course, with an electric toaster, must take what comes. Unless immediately hot-buttered, it must be stood on end to allow for the escape of steam while it cools; otherwise it will go flabby. For the same reason, crusts should be cut off *after* the toast is made, and not before.

It is sometimes thought that toast is less fattening than bread, but weight for weight, this is not so, as some of the water is driven off during toasting. Its pleasant flavour derives from the conversion of some of the starch in the bread to dextrin.

Fried Bread

Bread must be fried in *very hot* fat or cooking oil, as it will otherwise absorb too much of the cooking medium and become soggy and greasy. Fry it for about two minutes on each side until crisp and golden brown and up-end it briefly to drain off excess fat or oil.

A slice or half-slice of fried bread goes well with a variety of breakfast favourites, such as fried or scrambled eggs, grilled or fried bacon, fried chippolatas and mushrooms, or grilled tomatoes. Poached eggs are best served on hot-buttered toast.

Here is a recipe from 'Wyvern's' *Fifty Breakfasts* of 1894, which also makes an attractive dish for a light supper:

Ham Toast with Poached Eggs

4 slices bread	½oz (15g) butter
Cooking fat or oil	Spoonful gravy
2oz (60g) lean ham, cooked and minced	4 eggs

Cut four squares of bread a quarter of an inch thick and large enough to hold a poached egg each. Fry these crisply and brown, and keep hot. Pass sufficient lean ham through the mincing machine to yield a top-dressing for each 'toast', warm the mince in a small saucepan over a low fire, with half an ounce of butter, and moisten it with a spoonful of gravy or melted glaze. Keep this in the hot saucepan in a *bain-marie* while you poach the four eggs; when they are ready, spread the mixture on the fried bread, and place a poached egg on the surface of each, having trimmed the edges of the whites neatly all round. Send in quite hot.

Mushrooms on Toast

There is an art in cooking mushrooms. When grilled, they dry out, and if cooked slowly in a surplus of fat they absorb large quantities and ooze it. Perhaps the best method is to melt a modicum of bacon fat in a large non-stick pan and to fry the mushrooms at moderate temperature, shaking all the while. Serve on fried bread with grilled bacon.

Note: Tomatoes are much more watery than mushrooms; they tend to disintegrate when fried and are better grilled.

French Toast
French toast, especially when served with crisp grilled or fried bacon, is a meal in itself. There are two ways of making it.

Beat an egg with a teaspoonful of water on a large plate. Cut thick slices of bread, remove the crusts and place them in the beaten egg. Allow them to absorb as much as they will and to stand for five minutes, then fry in really hot fat or cooking oil until golden brown, turning them if you are not using deep fat.

Alternatively, toast the bread lightly on each side before dipping it into the beaten egg and fry at once in the hot fat or cooking oil. French toast made in this way absorbs less of the egg and is lighter and crisper on the outside. Both styles have their devotees.

Toasted Sandwich (Serves two)
This also makes an appetizing light lunch or supper.

3 oz (80 g) butter	*2 tomatoes, peeled and sliced*
4 thin slices bread	*4 lettuce leaves*
2 hard-boiled eggs, sliced	*Salt and pepper*
2 thin rounds cooked ham or	
6 rashers grilled bacon	
2 thin slices Cheddar cheese	

Melt the butter either on a griddle or on the hot plate of an electric cooker. If you have neither of these, you can make do with a heavy frying pan. Cut the crusts from the bread and brown on a gentle heat.

Meanwhile, have ready the hard-boiled eggs, the ham or grilled rashers of bacon, the slices of cheese, the sliced tomatoes and a few lettuce leaves.

When brown on one side, turn all the bread over and put more butter on the griddle. On two of the slices, place first the cheese, giving it time to melt a little, then the ham or grilled bacon, the lettuce, the rounds of hard-boiled egg and finally the tomatoes. Increase the heat as all four slices brown on the lower side.

Season with salt and pepper, cover with the second slices, cut the sandwiches in two and serve immediately.

Muffins

Muffins, a *sine qua non* of the Victorian breakfast table, are nowadays encountered, if at all, at tea-time; but one can hardly write a book about breakfasts without supplying a recipe. In his *Fifty Breakfasts*, 'Wyvern' suggests that the 'simplest possible system of baking' is with baking powder rather than yeast. This recipe will make eighteen small muffins:

1 lb (450g) flour   *1 pint (600ml) milk*
1 oz (30g) baking powder   *Butter*
Salt

Sift together a pound of fine flour, an ounce of Yeatman's powder [baking powder], and two saltspoonfuls of salt, stir in enough milk by degrees to form a smooth, but rather stiff, batter. Butter four muffin rings, lay them on a buttered baking sheet well heated, half fill them with the batter, and put them in the oven. When the batter has risen level with the top of the rings, turn them gently and bake till a good straw colour, then take out of the tin, turn the muffins out of the rings, open them, toast slightly on the inside, butter them, fold the pieces together again, and serve at once. About a pint of milk or a little more will probably be required to form the batter. Time, about twenty-five minutes.

Sally Lunns

Sally Lunns, the invention of an eighteenth-century English baker of that name, were regularly eaten at breakfast. Janie Ellice, whose recipe book dating from 1846-59 has recently been printed, obtained her receipt from

'O. BROOKE,
BREAD & BISCUIT BAKER,
NO. 28 BROAD STREET,
BATH (IF STILL ALIVE)'

and commented that, 'This is an excellent dish for Breakfast, though not often recommended by Doctors.'

The following recipe is taken from 'Wyvern's' *Fifty Breakfasts*:

1 lb (450g) flour   *2 eggs, beaten*
2 oz (60g) butter   *Milk*
½ oz (15g) baking powder   *A little sugar, if desired*
Salt

Rub the two ounces of butter into a pound of flour, with which half an ounce of baking powder has been thoroughly sifted and a saltspoonful of salt. Convert this into dough by first mixing with it two well-beaten eggs, and then milk enough by degrees to bring it to the consistency of thick batter. Put this into buttered muffin rings upon a hot buttered baking tin, and bake in a quick oven for fifteen minutes.

Waffles

Waffles are, of course, an American rather than a British breakfast speciality, but are so popular that it seems in place to give a recipe.

Makes 6 to 8

6oz (170g) flour
3 teaspoons baking powder
2 teaspoons sugar
½ teaspoon salt

½ pint (300ml) top of the milk
2 eggs, beaten
3 tablespoons melted butter

Sieve the flour and thoroughly mix it together with the baking powder, sugar and salt. Transfer to a bowl, add the milk, beaten eggs and melted butter and beat to form a thin batter, if necessary adding a little more milk.

Waffles are best cooked in an electric iron, which does not require greasing. Pour about a tablespoon of the batter into the centre of each compartment and allow it to spread out. Close the cover of the iron and cook until the steaming stops. At this point the waffles should be well puffed out and delicately brown. Remove with a fork and serve hot with melted butter, warm maple syrup and grilled bacon.

It is now possible to buy frozen, pre-fabricated waffles, which are simply toasted according to the directions on the package in an electric toaster — but, in our opinion, they are a poor substitute.

CHAPTER VII

Marmalade

CROISSANTS WITH HONEY, or simply with creamy country butter, are very nice (over the other preserves or sweetened compôtes served with breakfast abroad, it is better to draw a veil) but no British breakfast worthy of the name is complete without toast and marmalade. There is just no substitute for the bitter-sweet tang of marmalade made with Seville oranges, though oddly enough it seems out of place at any meal except breakfast.

There is a story that marmalade was first concocted by Mary Queen of Scots' Spanish doctor as a cure for sea-sickness and hence called *mer malade*, but this bears all the marks of a mere *conte*. Much more likely is that it took its name from the Portuguese *mermelada*, a stiff paste made from quinces and usually served with cheese, with which it goes excellently. In Spain, a similar confection is known as *membrillo* and was a great favourite of the last of the Anti-Popes, Pedro de Luna, so much so that his enemies made an unsuccessful attempt to kill him by dosing it with arsenic and serving it to him in his castle at Peñiscola.

Marmalade, as we know it today, originated in Scotland. In his *Tours of Scotland*, published in 1760, Bishop Pococke observes that at breakfast 'there is always, besides butter and toasted bread, honey and jelly of currants and preserved orange peel'. Whether or not this was the preserve we now know, it seems that orange marmalade was first made on any scale by Janet Pierson in Dundee during the latter years of the eighteenth century. A well-founded story relates how a ship with a cargo of oranges from Seville took shelter in the harbour. Janet's husband, James Keiller, bought a large quantity at bargain price, only to find that the fruit was too bitter to re-sell. His thrifty wife decided to experiment and converted it into an orange jam, which proved such a success that

Lettering from a Keiller marmalade jar, current during the last quarter of the nineteenth century and until 1914

there was a runaway demand, and in 1797 the firm of James Keiller & Son was established to make and market it.

By the 1870's two other family concerns in Scotland were making orange marmalade. With help from the Duke of Gordon, Margaret Baxter, whose husband was one of the fifty gardeners, set up a shop in Fochabers on the Moray Firth for selling her home-made jams; and from this has sprung the great modern firm of Baxters of Speyside, one of whose specialities is a marmalade flavoured with whisky. Down in Paisley, another couple, the Robinsons, came up with another version, a clear jelly with finely-shredded peel, now known as 'Golden Shred'.

The manufacture of marmalade was also begun in England, where in 1874, Sarah Jane, wife of the Oxford grocer Frank Cooper, began making it from a family recipe in the kitchens of the old Angel Hotel and selling it to the dons from her husband's shop in the High. The taste for their coarse-cut, dark marmalade quickly spread to the undergraduates, who had soon christened it 'Squish' and were consuming it by the jarful at 'brekker'.

Demand rapidly outpaced the facilities of the hotel kitchen, and before long the local newspapers were hailing Oxford Marmalade and the new

Frank Cooper's Victoria Marmalade manufactory in Oxford c. 1900

premises in which it was made as one of the town's great tourist attractions:

> The Manufactory in Victoria Buildings near the Railway Stations, ranks as one of the sights of Oxford, and visitors cannot do better than spend half an hour going over these extensive works. They never fail to be struck by the scrupulously clean and hygienic arrangements as well as the up-to-date appliances by which the "OXFORD" Marmalade is manufactured....
>
> ... It is a veritable 'Varsity institution, and is used by members of the University crews while in training. The first thing that strikes the eye of the "Fresher" upon his arrival in Oxford is the imposing front of the Victoria factory, and the next morning he will make the acquaint-

ance of this delicious preserve at "brekker". In Oxford at least it is the autocrat of the breakfast table.

And not only in Oxford, as the paper points out in a paean of local pride: 'Amongst the nobilities who are patrons of this delectable delicacy are H.R.H. Princess Christian, H.E. The Viceroy of India, Lily, Duchess of Marlborough, the Bishop of London, Viscount Valentia, and scores of Peers and Peeresses, and nearly all the Naval and Military Messes.'

Although marmalades made from limes and lemons are now popular, the traditional chunky variety, such as Frank Cooper's Coarse Cut, is still made from Seville oranges. Bitter oranges were introduced to Spain by the Moors long before the returning Crusaders first encountered them in Italy and Sicily (sweet oranges made their appearance in Europe later and were brought from the Far East by the Portuguese). The trees, with their

The interior of Frank Cooper's grocery in High Street, Oxford c. 1900

sweet-scented blossom, dark green leaves and glowing fruit, line the streets and patios of Seville and Córdoba, and the orange groves stretch for miles outside. Ninety-five per cent of the crop from Seville is exported to Britain, either as fresh oranges or as a processed pulp.

Since 1960 much of the preparation of Frank Cooper's Coarse Cut marmalade has been carried out in Seville itself soon after picking, so retaining the aromatic quality of the fruit. Only the best and largest oranges are selected and they undergo a preliminary cooking at near boiling point, so that the pungent oils in the inside and in the outer skin of the fruit permeate the thick flesh of the peel. The oranges are then quartered, the centre pith removed and the flesh separated from the peel, which is cut into thick chunks some ¼ inch wide. Cooking proper takes place in four stages by traditional methods in unpressurized pans: first, the heart of the fruit is boiled without sugar or peel; next, the fruit and peel are cooked together and then left to mature for three months, or as much as a year for 'vintage marmalades' (this was one of the secrets of Frank Cooper's original method). At this stage the cooked fruit is despatched in barrels to England, where it is stored until required. Part of the sugar is now added, and the whole mass is cooked together and left to marinate for a few days. It is finally brought up to the correct degree of sweetness with addition of further sugar and undergoes a last boiling, again in open pans, to concentrate and refine the flavour. The end result of this careful and time-consuming process is a rich, dark, bitter-sweet marmalade, differing from most in its thick chunks of aromatic peel.

Other manufacturers have their own methods — the Robinsons, for example, set out in the first place to make a sweeter, more jelly-like preserve with the peel finely sliced. And it is, of course, possible to make your own marmalade (see recipes, page 101). In our own house in Scotland, the marathon jam and marmalade-making, like that of Christmas puddings, was one of the fixed festivals of the domestic calendar, and, according to season, the kitchen would be fragrant with the aromas of hot sugar and the steaming cauldrons of bitter oranges or raspberries.

Marmalade was traditionally sold in stoneware jars, with a salt glaze vitrified at some 1200°C. They were easily sterilized in boiling water and ideal for preserves generally.

The earliest jars, known as 'galley-pots', sloped outwards a little from base to rim, so that covers could be tied on more securely, but were replaced during the eighteenth century by the now familiar jam-jar with straight sides and moulded rim. When the cheaper and equally hygienic

BREAKFAST *and* SUPPER DISHES

C. HERMAN SENN

INSPECTING CHEF

OF THE

NATIONAL SCHOOL OF COOKERY

The cover of C. Herman Senn's Breakfast and Supper Dishes, *c. 1890*

Canadian Pacific

*The Tall 'Penny-farthing' Bicycle
became very popular in England
and North America between 1872-1889.*

Breakfast

Chilled Juices : V8 Vegetable Grape Fruit Orange Tomato
Chilled Melons : Spanish, Water
Sliced Pineapple
Grape Fruit Apples Oranges Pears
Grapes Tangerines Plums
Compôtes : Prunes Raisins Figs Plums Apricots Peaches
Baked Apples (Hot or Cold)

Special : Clam Broth French Onion Soup

Rolled Oats Cream of Wheat Oatmeal Porridge
Rice Krispies Shredded Wheat Grape Nuts Bran Flakes
Wheat Flakes Pep Puffed Rice Weet-a-Bix
Wheat Germ Tonic

Fried Fillet of Whiting au Citron
Grilled Butterfish au Beurre
Findon Haddock in Cream

Eggs : Boiled, Fried, Turned, Poached, Scrambled, Country Style
Omelettes : Plain, Savoury, Cheese, Tomato, Pimento, Jam
Broiled Breakfast Bacon
Fried Pork Sausages Hashed Lamb with Pickled Walnuts
Purée Potatoes

TO ORDER
Windsor Bacon Small Steak Fried Tomatoes Devilled Beef Bones

COLD
Roast Beef Leicester Brawn Jellied Ox Tongue
Lettuce Tomato Radishes

Raisin or Plain Buckwheat Cakes with Honey or Maple Syrup
Waffles with Demerara Sugar
Rolls : White, Graham *Breads* : Raisin, Energen, Hovis
Muffins : Corn, Bran *Biscuits* : Ry-vita, Vita Weat
Toasts White, Brown, Raisin, Melba *To Order* : French Toast
Croissants Danish Pastries Brioches
Fruit Buns

Conserves Marmalades Honey (Cloudy or Clear)

Teas: Ceylon China Green Camomile Mint
Coffee: Sanka Cona Nescafé
Instant Postum
Cocoa Yogurt Chocolate Buttermilk

EMPRESS OF CANADA Tuesday, February 6, 1962

S78: Printed in England. P/AG.

A menu from R.M.S. Empress of Canada, *February 6, 1962*

Frank Cooper's Marmalade manufactory, Oxford:
(above) *The boiling room, 1903*
(below) *Cutting up the fruit, c. 1900*

Packing jars of marmalade at Frank Cooper's Victoria Marmalade manufactory, c. 1900

— but less decorative — glass jars came on to the market, the stone jars began to disappear and have now become collectors' items, fetching several pounds apiece at sales. *Antiques & Art Weekly* has recently (September 10, 1977) devoted an article to the subject.

The first stoneware marmalade jars were introduced by James Keiller and Son on their inception in 1797, and the firm for long continued to use handmade pottery containers with a bold legend in black. Crosse and Blackwell, with whom Keillers were later incorporated, obtained their jars from Doulton and Co., but after 1940 they were replaced by an opalescent white glass jar, very similar in appearance but surface-printed instead of on the slip. Other well-known concerns, such as W. P. Hartley, whose trademark was a lighthouse with waves curling on the rocks at the bottom, Wilkins and Son of Tiptree fame, Chivers and Smedleys, bought their pots from equally famous potteries.

When Sarah Jane Cooper began making marmalade at the Angel in Oxford, she sold only 182 lbs in the first year and 340 lbs in the second and probably made do with plain or re-used pots. By 1902, when she retired and the move was made to the Victoria Works, production was running at 100,000 lbs a year, and until 1941 the firm was supplied with stoneware by Maling of Newcastle-on-Tyne. In 1-lb, 2-lb, 3-lb and 7-lb catering sizes, the jars were most handsome objects, emblazoned with the Royal Coat of Arms. Nineteenth-century domestics would certainly have been incredulous had they known that the simple marmalade jar was to become the subject of scholarly articles and to be sought after simply for its decorative value.

Early pottery jars used for Frank Cooper's Oxford marmalade

It is entirely appropriate that Oxford should have made such a memorable contribution to the breakfast table, since 'brekker' was a University institution, and it seems in place to end this chapter on marmalade with Thomas Hughes's description of 'A Breakfast at Drysdale's' from *Tom Brown at Oxford*:

No man in St Ambrose College gave such breakfasts as Drysdale. Not the great heavy spread for thirty or forty which came once or twice a term, when everything was supplied out of the college kitchen, and you had to ask leave of the Dean before you could have it at all. In those ponderous feasts the most humble of undergraduates might rival the most artistic, if he could only pay his battel bill, or get credit with the cook. But the daily morning meal, when even gentlemen commoners were limited to two hot dishes out of the kitchen, this was Drysdale's forte. Ordinary men left the matter in the hands of scouts, and were content with the ever recurring buttered toast and eggs, with a dish of broiled ham, or something of that sort, and marmalade and bitter ale to finish with; but Drysdale was not an ordinary man, as you felt in a moment when you went to breakfast with him for the first time.

The staircase on which he lived was inhabited, except in the garrets, by men of the fast set, and he and three others, who had an aversion to solitary feeding, had established a breakfast club....

Every morning the boy from the Weirs arrived with freshly caught gudgeon, and now and then an eel or trout, which the scouts on the staircase had learnt to cook delicately in oil. Fresh watercress came in the same basket, and the college kitchen furnished a spitchcocked chicken, or grilled turkey's leg. In the season there were plover's eggs; or, at the worst, there was a dainty omelette; and a distant baker, famed for his light rolls and high charges, sent in the bread, the common domestic college loaf being of course out of the question... Then there would be a deep Yorkshire pie, or reservoir of potted game, as a *pièce de résistance*, and three or four sorts of preserves; and a large cool tankard of cider or ale cup to finish with, or soda water and maraschino for a change. Tea and coffee were there indeed, but merely as a complement to those respectable beverages, for they were rarely touched by the breakfasters of No. 3 staircase. Pleasant young gentlemen they were... and they might have had potted hippopotamus for breakfast if they had chosen to order it, which they would most likely have done if they had thought of it....

Sunt lacrimae rerum; the groves of Academe are no longer as fresh and green as yester-year.

> Stands the Church clock at ten to three?
> And is there honey still for tea?

Or do those pewter-covered platters with the jugged hare and devilled kidneys come smoking from the college kitchen?
We very much doubt it.

MARMALADE

In an age when most women have their hands full with looking after the house and family or going out to a job of their own, few have the time to make their own jams and marmalades. Those who wish to try cannot do better than with the following traditional recipes, two from Elizabeth Acton's *Modern Cookery for Private Families*, first published in 1845.

This orange marmalade is dark and rather bitter.

Genuine Scotch Marmalade

   3 lb (1·4 kg) Seville oranges   *6 lb (2·7 kg) sugar*
   3 quarts (1·7 litres) water

Take some bitter [Seville] oranges, and double their weight of sugar; cut the rind of the fruit into quarters and peel it off, and if the marmalade be not wanted very thick, take off some of the spongy white skin inside the rind. Cut the chips as thin as possible, and about half an inch long, and divide the pulp into small bits, removing carefully the seeds, which may be steeped in part of the water that is to make the marmalade, and which must be in the proportion of a quart to a pound of fruit. Put the chips and pulp into a deep earthenware dish, and pour the water boiling over them; let them remain for twelve or fourteen hours, and then turn the whole into the preserving pan, and boil it until the chips are perfectly tender. When they are so, add by degrees the sugar (which should be previously pounded), and boil it until it jellies. The water in which the seeds have been steeped, and which must be taken from the quantity apportioned to the whole of the preserve, should be poured into a hair-sieve, and the seeds well worked in it with the back of a spoon; a strong clear jelly will be obtained by this means, which must be washed off them by pouring their own liquor through the sieve in small portions over them. This must be added to the fruit when it is first set on the fire.

Quince Marmalade

   4 lb (1·8 kg) quinces, pared   *3 lb (1·35 kg) sugar*
   and cored
   1 quart (1·14 litres) prepared
   quince juice

When to economize the fruit is not an object, pare, core, and quarter some of the inferior quinces, and boil them in as much water as will nearly cover them, until they begin to break. Strain the juice from them and for the marmalade put half a pint of it to each pound of fresh quinces; in preparing these, be careful to cut out the hard stone parts round the cores. Simmer them gently until they are perfectly tender, then press them, with the juice, through a coarse sieve; put them into a perfectly clean pan, and boil them until they form almost a dry paste. Add for each pound of quinces and the half-pint of juice, three-quarters of a pound of sugar in a fine powder, and boil the marmalade for half an hour, stirring it gently without ceasing; it will be very firm and bright in colour. If made shortly after the fruit is gathered, a little additional sugar will be required; and when a richer and less dry marmalade is better liked, it must be boiled for a shorter time, and an equal weight of fruit and sugar may be used.

Grapefruit Marmalade

A recipe from F. Marian McNeill's *Book of Breakfasts*.

4 *grapefruits*	*Sugar as below*
4 *lemons*	

Put four grapefruits into a saucepan with sufficient cold water to cover them, bring to the boil and cook slowly until the fruit is tender and can easily be pierced with a fork. Remove the pan from the fire, and leave it to stand as it is overnight. Take four lemons, wash them, cut them in halves, squeeze out the juice and strain into a basin. Add the pips, tied in a piece of muslin, together with the rind of the lemon sliced thinly. Pour over this two quarts of water and leave it also to stand overnight.

Next day, drain the grapefruits from the water (which may be thrown away), cut them in halves, scoop out all the pulp and put into the preserving pan with the juice of the grapefruits and lemons. Boil this slowly until reduced by half. Measure the fruit, and to each pint allow a pound and a half of sugar. Reboil, add the sugar, stir constantly until it has dissolved, then boil slowly for one hour to one and a half, or until the marmalade will set when tried on a cold saucer. Put into jars and tie down when cold.

Orange Jelly

4 lb (1·8 kg) Seville oranges   Sugar as below
2 lemons

Wash and dry the oranges and lemons, grate off the rinds and reserve. Remove and discard the thick white skin remaining on the fruit, cut the flesh into small pieces and put in a preserving pan with 4½ pints (2· 7 litres) of cold water. Bring to the boil and simmer for thirty minutes with frequent stirring. Pour into a jelly bag and leave to drip overnight or strain through a piece of muslin placed inside a sieve. When straining is complete, measure the amount of liquid, pour into a preserving pan and add the grated rind, together with the sugar in the proportion of 1 lb (450 g) to each pint of liquid. Stir, bring to the boil and continue slow boiling until a sample placed on a cold saucer sets to a firm jelly.

CHAPTER VIII

The Grateful Liquors

'...the board with cups and spoons is crown'd,
The berries crackle, and the mill turns round;
On shining altars of Japan they raise
The silver lamp; the fiery spirits blaze;
From silver spouts the grateful liquors glide,
While China's earth receives the smoaking tide...'
Alexander Pope, *The Rape of the Lock*

OVER THE CENTURIES, and frequently during the last, what the British drank at breakfast were liquors in the modern sense of the word. Tea, coffee and chocolate were not introduced to Britain until the middle of the seventeenth century and for long after that were too expensive to be drunk by labouring people, whose habitual beverage was ale.

That lively-minded physician Dr Andrew Borde put things in a nutshell when he wrote in his *Breviary of Diet*, first published in England in 1547: 'Water is not wholesome sole by itself for an Englishman. Good wine moderately drunk doth actuate and doth quicken a man's wits; it doth comfort his heart; it doth scour the liver; it doth engender good blood; it doth comfort and nourish the brain, wherefore it is medicinal.'

'I myself,' he continues, 'which am a physician, cannot away with water, wherefore I do leave all water, and do take myself to good ale, and otherwhile for ale I do take good Gascon wine, but I will not drink strong wines. Mean wines, as wines of Gascony, French wines is good with meats, specially claret wine' — and for hundreds of years, claret, and more particularly ale, were the regular drinks at breakfast.

'Ale,' as Charles Cooper observes in *The English Table in History and Literature*, 'was an early English passion. It was drunk in mighty draughts by our Saxon and Danish ancestors; it was specified among the liquors provided for a royal banquet by the saintly Edward the Confessor, and the price of it was regulated by enactment of our Norman conquerors.' As drunk then, it was little more than a 'sweet wurt' made by steeping malted wheat or barley in water, and the hops which give it the refreshing bitter tang were unknown to British brewers until the beginning of the sixteenth century, although they had been used by the Germans two hundred years earlier.

The distinction between ale and beer is sometimes imprecise. It has often been said that beer is a form of ale flavoured with hops; but originally the difference seems to have been in the type of malt from which they were brewed. Ale was made from malted grain dried at a low temperature and was consequently light in colour, whereas beer derived its darker colour and characteristic taste from malts heated more strongly and partially charred.

'The Drinking Party', Thomas Rowlandson

In the early eighteenth century the most popular malt liquors were ale, beer and 'twopenny', and it was the custom to call for a tankard of 'half-and-half' ale and beer. An enterprising brewer, Harwood, then began selling beer in barrels, which combined all three; and it was this which became known as 'porter', since it was so popular among labourers. With the emergence of the large Burton brewers, such as Worthington, Bass and Allsopp, in the late eighteenth century, the terms became blurred; and today 'ale' and 'beer' are virtually synonymous. It is perhaps of interest that in times past there was no compunction about serving beer to children; and in 1704 the Children's Diet at Christ Church Hospital in London consisted of bread and beer for breakfast every day.

As late as 1862, Tovey was still recommending 'good, sound claret' as 'an agreeable substitute for tea or coffee at breakfast during warm weather'. Even Dylan Thomas's Sir Gregory Grig was compelled to admit that the stronger wines quaffed by our ancestors — port, sack (sherry), tent (Madeira) and 'mountain wine' (Málaga) — were too hard on the liver in the morning, and claret was, after all, the natural choice.

As its French derivation, '*clairet*', implies, it is a light, clear, refreshing wine; and further than this a particularly 'English' one. From 1152, when the town of Bordeaux and the Duchy of Guyenne passed into the possession of Henry II as part of the dowry of his wife, Eleanor of Aquitaine, until 1451, the Bordelais was English territory and most of its wine was shipped to Britain. Thereafter, it became more of a Scots drink than an English thanks to the Auld Alliance, and, in the words of P. Morton Shand, 'the Scots gentry continued to drink claret, which they usually shipped direct to Leith, Dundee, Montrose or Aberdeen from Bordeaux, with or without benison of the Excise, long after English country squires were suffering agonies of gout from Methuen port in order to boycott everything French and see "Boney to Blazes"'. Dr Johnson voiced the eighteenth-century English contempt for claret in describing it as 'a boy's' or 'intellectual' wine; but it regained its popularity during the nineteenth century, though often suffering from what was significantly known as '*travail à l'anglais*' — blending with darker, stronger wine for vitiated English palates.

When all is said and done, there is something to be said for drinking a light wine with breakfast in hot weather. As a young man, sharing living-quarters in a garage in Laurel Canyon with some other Hollywood hopefuls, I [J. R.] well remember the carboys of pleasant Californian red, with which we used to wash down our ham and eggs!

A wine merchant's list of 1887. The prices are per dozen

BARTON & CO.,
Wine Merchants & Shippers,

CHIEF OFFICES: 59, ST. JAMES' STREET, LONDON, S.W.,
Where all Correspondence should be addressed.

CITY OFFICES AND CELLARS: 17, GRACECHURCH STREET, E.C.,
AND ST. MILDRED'S COURT, POULTRY, E.C.

Champagne.	Vintage 1878 and 1880.						
	70/-	72/-	74/-	78/-	84/-	96/-	100/-
	According to date of landing, quantity, and degree of excellence.						

Also a large Stock of 1874 choice branded Champagnes, from 100/- to 180/- per doz.

Claret.	Light Dinner.	Higher Class—First, Second, & Third Growths.					
		1878	1876	1879	1877	1872	1873	1875
	18/- to 30/-	36/-	42/-	48/-	54/-	60/-	66/-	72/-

Also a large Stock of Latour, Leoville, Barton, and Lafite, 1864, 1871, 1875.

Sherry.	Pale, Pale Dry, Superior Pale.	Gold, Brown, Amber.	Manzanillas, Montillas, Vino de Pastos, Amontillados.	Old in Bottle of all the choicest varieties.
	21/- to 42/-	24/- to 54/-	32/- to 72/-	84/- to 140/- According to age and character.

Port.	Light or full-bodied.	Choice, Dry, Rich, & excellent flavour, from the wood and old in bottle.	Fine Natural.	VINTAGES. 1820, 1834, 1840, 1847, 1851, 1853, 1854, 1863, 1870.
	20/- to 36/-	40/- to 60/-	48/- to 72/-	

Chablis, Sauterne, Madeira, Hock, Moselle, Marsala, Burgundy, Brandy, Whisky, and Liqueurs.

CUSTOMERS VISITING LONDON FOR SHORT PERIODS CAN HAVE THEIR CELLARS STOCKED ON SALE OR RETURN.

Decanted bottles of Claret, &c., for tasting, sent on receipt of telegram or letter.

BARTON & CO.'S HOUSE HAS BEEN ESTABLISHED OVER 100 YEARS.

Coffee, which at the time came exclusively from Arabia, was first popularised in England by the coffee houses, the first of which opened in Oxford in 1650, perhaps as an outcome of the coffee-drinking habits of Conopios, an acolyte of the murdered Cyrill, Patriarch of Constantinople, who was given sanctuary at Balliol College.

The first London coffee house was opened in 1652 by Pasqua Rosée, a native of Ragusa (it is probably no coincidence that it was through Venice that coffee was first brought to Europe) in St Michael's Alley, Cornhill. Others, such as Will's, Garraway's, Slaughter's, Button's, the Grecian, Tom's and Don Saltero's rapidly sprang up and became known as 'penny universities', since for the price of a penny one might enter their smoke-laden premises and rub shoulders with a Johnson, Burke, Garrick, Reynolds, Dryden, Swift, Pepys or other literary, artistic and political luminaries of the day. It was, of course, in coffee houses that the *Spectator*, *Tatler* and Lloyds of London were born; and a more dubious legacy is that of the tip—brass-bound boxes with the words TO INSURE PROMPTNESS being set up to receive contributions for the waiters.

Opposition to the coffee houses came from the innkeepers and also from wives abandoned by their coffee-drinking spouses. A tract appeared entitled '*The Women's Petition Against Coffee*, representing to public consideration the grand inconvenience accruing to their Sex from the excessive use of the drying and enfeebling Liquor', and the ladies complained that coffee made men as 'unfruitful as the deserts where that unhappy berry is said to be bought'. (Could this have been because their husbands spent more time with their coffee-drinking cronies than in the marital bed?)

But coffee had won the day; by 1715 over 2000 London coffee houses' catered to all classes of society, and more coffee was drunk in London than in any other city in the world. First sold by apothecaries in the form of green beans as a cure-for-all-ills, it was not long before it invaded the breakfast table, where it was usually drunk black and unsweetened, but sometimes mixed with mustard, cinnamon, cloves, spearmint, molasses, sugar or sour cream.

A firm favourite with the English upper classes as a breakfast and dinner beverage, coffee has never in Britain enjoyed quite the universal appeal that it does in the United States — though there are signs that, with the advent of instant coffee, it is well on the way to doing so.

The reasons for this are that, until a much later period, it was expensive compared with the ale drunk by working people and was soon to be challenged by tea. In 1700, when tea was a costly and exotic drink served mainly in the better coffee houses, only some 800,000 lbs were imported; a century later the figure had risen to over 7,000,000 lbs a year.

Tea was known in China for centuries B.C. and poetically described by Taoist alchemists as 'froth of the liquid jade' (its more mundane name was Ch'a, hence the English slang 'char'), but it was not systematically cultivated until about 350 A.D. Its history is bound up with that of the British Empire (how many commodities have contributed to the loss of a great colonial territory, as did the tax on tea in North America?) and more particularly with the rise and fall of the East India Company, which, more than a government trading agency, became the ruling body of British India.

The Company's agents were interested in tea as long ago as 1615, when its factor in Hirado wrote to his colleague in Macao, requesting 'a pot of the best sort of chaw'—apparently unaware that it was plentifully

An advertisement for tea, 1885

available in Japan, where he was stationed. It was not until 1657 that it was first sold publicly in England, at Garraway's coffee house, when the proprietor assured his customers that the Chinese valued it at 'twice its weight in silver', going on to claim for it all the virtues of a new and exotic beverage: 'It vanquisheth heavy dreams, easeth the Brain, and strengtheneth the Memory.'

This first sample came from Dutch sources, and although, at the beginning of her reign in 1702, Queen Anne substituted tea for ale at breakfast, using a large, bell-shaped silver teapot rather than the tiny china pots then in fashion, it was not until the middle of the century that it was obtainable by any but the wealthy. By then, as Macaulay writes in his *Life of Johnson*, 'The old philosopher . . . in the brown coat with the metal buttons and the shirt which ought to be at the wash, [was] blinking, puffing, rolling his head, drumming with his fingers, tearing his meat like a tiger, and swallowing his tea in oceans.'

It seems that there was a variety of reasons for the eventual triumph of

SO LIKELY!

SCENE—*Bar of a Railway Refreshment Room.*

Barmaid. "TEA, SIR?"   *Mr. Boozy.* "TEA!!! ME!!!!"

A gentleman with no use for the 'coffee taverns' (cartoon by Phil May,
Punch, 1895)

tea in England. The East India Company had lost out to its French and
Dutch competitors over imports of coffee and had a vested interest in
importing tea from its establishments in China, for long the only supplier,
and was abetted by a government that viewed the coffee houses as a
hotbed of political dissension. Although the preparation of tea for the

market was more complex than that of coffee — involving the withering, rolling and firing of the leaves — once in the hands of the consumer, there was no need for the ritual of roasting and grinding. All that was necessary was the addition of boiling water. Again, after the abolition of the East India Company's monopoly, the speedy tea clippers, with their slim lines and press of canvas, afforded a much improved means of transport.

Tea-drinking became universal in Britain only after the discovery of wild tea plants in India. The first shipments of native Indian tea caused a sensation, and in the face of efforts by the East India Company to preserve its monopoly and to keep prices artificially high, plantations in Assam were largely developed by private companies with the support of London merchants such as W. J. and H. Thompson, Joseph Travers and Sons and the Messrs Twining. With the progressive demise of the East India Company as a trading concern, its dissolution after the Indian Mutiny in 1857 and the subsequent establishment of plantations in Ceylon and Java, Britain was on the way to becoming the nation of tea-drinkers that it is today.

Among the working classes its consumption was encouraged by the

One of the 'coffee taverns' for working men, established in the 1870s
and serving early-morning coffee, tea or cocoa instead of spirits
(contemporary engraving)

growth of 'coffee taverns' in the 1870s, providing coffee, tea or cocoa at the beginning of the day, and designed as an alternative to the public houses, with their cheap gin and spirits. At the end of the century enlightened Quaker firms, such as Cadbury's and Fry's, were serving tea and biscuits free of charge to girls who turned up early for work. By a full turn of the circle, the 'tea-break' has now become notorious.

Coffee, tea and chocolate all made their first bow in the coffee houses. Here is Christopher Anstey on a 'Public Breakfast' in the *New Bath Guide* of 1766:

> You may go to Carlisle's, and to Almack's too;
> And I'll give you my head if you find such a host,
> For coffee, tea, chocolate, butter, and toast:
> How he welcomes at once all the world and his wife,
> And how civil to folk he ne'er saw in his life.

There is as much of a mystique about the early history of chocolate as of that of tea. Cocoa beans were first brought to Europe by Columbus in 1494, and Cortez, during his conquest of Mexico in 1519, noted that the Aztecs believed that *chocolatl*, as the ground bean was called, was a gift to man from the gods. Writing in 1568, Bernal Diaz del Castillo alludes to a fermented liquor made from cocoa and used by Montezuma: 'After the hot dishes (300 in number) had been removed from Montezuma's dinner-table, every now and then was handed to him a golden pitcher filled with a kind of liquor made from Cocoa, which is of a very exciting nature. The beverage was also presented to the monarch by women, with the greatest veneration.'

For about a century after its introduction to Spain, the Spaniards kept the secret of its preparation, but a chocolate factory was established in Italy in 1606, and from Italy or Spain knowledge of chocolate passed to France, where it became popular at the court of Louis XIV. One of the earliest records of its consumption in England is an advertisement which appeared in the *Public Advertiser* of Tuesday, June 16, 1657, to the effect that 'in Bishopgate Street, in Queen's Head Alley, at a Frenchman's house, is an excellent West India drink called Chocolate to be sold, where you may have it ready at any time, and also unmade at reasonable rates'.

In his *Curiosities of Literature*, Isaac d'Israeli comments that 'We had chocolate houses in London long after coffee houses; they seemed to have associated something more elegant and refined in their new term when

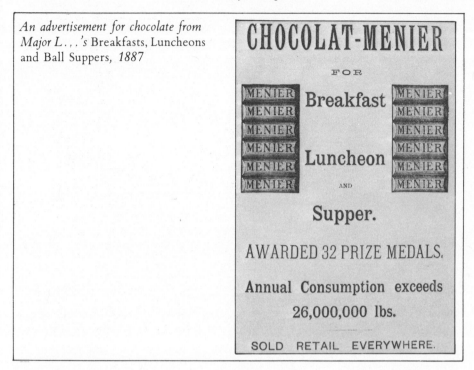

An advertisement for chocolate from Major L.,.'s Breakfasts, Luncheons and Ball Suppers, *1887*

the other had become common.' Some, with a select patronage, such as White's, which opened in St James's Street in 1698; the famous Tory 'Chocolate House' of Queen Anne's reign; and the 'Cocoa Tree', frequented by the *literati*, closed their doors to the public and were the forerunners of the exclusive London clubs of today.

Chocolate, which differs from cocoa in undergoing a further stage of manufacture during which the cocoa extract is mixed with sugar and finely milled, was a popular breakfast drink during the eighteenth and early nineteenth centuries. It seems from books such as Woodforde's *Diary of a Country Parson* that it was usually taken with toast, its substance and nourishment militating against its consumption with the heavy breakfasts enjoyed by a Mr Jorrocks.

Cocoa has always been a more plebeian beverage and a favourite at schools for assuaging hungry children. Although nothing made from cocoa beans is now cheap, one can perhaps leave the last word to the nineteenth-century author of a work on the *Commercial Products of the Vegetable Kingdom*: 'Cocoa is of domestic drinks the most alimentary; it is

'Enjoying their morning cocoa'
(advertisement from C. Herman
Senn's Ideal Breakfast Dishes,
Savouries and Curries, *c. 1890)*

"Yes, you're quite right! There is something about VAN HOUTEN'S that seems wanting in other Cocoas. I like its exquisite NATURAL flavour and its agreeable lightness. But what surprises me more than anything is its real economy. You only want just the smallest half teaspoonful to make a cup of delicious Cocoa. As for its value as a food you need only look at the children! They simply thrive on VAN HOUTEN'S."

without exception the cheapest food that we can conceive, as it may be literally termed meat and drink, and were our half-starved artizans and over-worked factory children induced to drink it, instead of the innutritive beverage called tea, its nutritive qualities would soon develop themselves in their improved looks and more robust condition.'

COFFEE, TEA AND CHOCOLATE

Coffee
Coffee now comes from a variety of sources, some of the best being Blue Mountain (Jamaica), Bogotá (Colombia), the Yemen, Costa Rica, Kenya and Brazil; and breakfast coffees are usually a blend. The somewhat bitter taste of most Continental coffees results from roasting the beans at a higher temperature, and also from the addition of chicory.

As important as the variety of coffee is its proper making. Many people now use ready-ground coffee, vacuum packed in tins, and it is essential that, once opened, the tins should be kept firmly closed. The best results are still obtained by using freshly roasted beans, and only as much should be ground as is needed for immediate use.

There are numerous ways of making coffee. The simplest and most traditional is to allow a tablespoon of medium-ground coffee per person and to place it in a heated coffee pot. Pour boiling water over it, stir briefly and allow to settle. It should then be poured carefully off the grounds and into the cup through a strainer. A variant is to heat the coffee in a small saucepan with cold water, adding a pinch of salt and milk if desired, until the grounds rise to the top. Remove at once from the fire, repeat twice, settle the grounds by adding a few drops of cold water, and strain off into the cups or a hot coffee pot.

There are, of course, a great variety of automatic coffee-making machines on the market, such as the well-known Cona and Russell-Hobbs, some functioning with filter papers and others by percolating hot water through a bed of ground coffee. Coffee made in a percolator tends to be slightly bitter; but the really important thing is never to boil or reheat it, when it loses its freshness and aroma.

There is a degree of snobbism about instant coffee. Certainly the cheaper powdered brands bear little resemblance to the real thing, but coffee made from the best freeze-dried granules is often first-rate.

Tea
Tea, like coffee, is now grown in a variety of countries, the main difference in style and flavour being between China tea, with its aromatic fragrance and delicacy, and that from India (of which the most delicate is from Darjeeling) and Ceylon.

Teas are broadly classified as the light, unfermented *Green*, drunk without milk or sugar, the partially fermented *Oolong*, and *Black*. In order of quality they are further graded as *Flowery Orange Pekoe*, *Broken Orange Pekoe*, *Orange Pekoe*, *Pekoe*, *Pekoe Souchong* and *Souchong*. Pekoes are made from the smaller leaves and *Souchongs* from the larger and coarser.

Tea should be kept in an air-tight tin or caddy (from the Malayan *kati*, a measurement of weight, perhaps refering to the bulk density of the contents) and made with water drawn freshly from the tap. If made with water which has been previously heated or boiled, it will taste flat and stale. First heat the pot thoroughly with boiling water, add a small teaspoon of dry tea per person (and 'one for the pot', if you like it

115

stronger), pour in freshly boiling water, stir, and allow to stand for a few minutes. If it infuses for too long an undue amount of tannin is extracted and it becomes bitter and astringent.

It can, of course, be made with tea-bags; but the snag is that water poured over a tea-bag in a cold cup soon cools and the flavour is not fully extracted. If you *must* use tea-bags, put them in a preheated teapot, pour in the boiling water and stir gently to allow the tea to infuse. A convenience of tea-bags is that they facilitate the disposal of the used tea-leaves—the conventional wisdom is that tea-leaves clog the waste-pipe while coffee grounds scour it— but it is quite simple to pour the used leaves into a small sieve and put them into the bin.

Chocolate

Allow an ounce of powdered 'drinking chocolate' to half a pint of milk. Heat the milk in a saucepan and slowly add the chocolate powder, stirring all the time. Remove from the fire just before the milk boils — at this point small bubbles will form at the surface of the liquid around the circumference of the pan—and continue stirring for a little longer. Sweeten to taste and serve at once. Unlike coffee, chocolate may be reheated without spoiling the flavour.

Cocoa

Cocoa is not as attractive a drink as chocolate—how many of us have suffered from it when made with water at school?—but can be quite palatable when properly made in a saucepan with rich milk.

Allow two teaspoons of cocoa powder to half a pint of full cream milk. First make a paste with a little of the milk, then add the remainder of the milk, stir well and bring to the boil. Sweeten with sugar and serve piping hot.

CHAPTER IX

Breakfast à la Mode

'THE CRITICAL PERIOD in matrimony,' wrote A. P. Herbert, 'is breakfast time.' He was of a generation when breakfast was a serious business taken *en famille*, with father's attention divided between *The Times* and his bacon and eggs, the children nervous about unfinished homework, and mother holding an uneasy balance.

But times have changed: father is off to the office by an early train and is lucky to get a boiled egg; somewhat later the children swallow their 'sunshine breakfast' of cereal and milk before being whisked off to school by car; while the teenager lives in a world of his own.

If awakened before midday, a somnolent, tousle-haired figure in a dressing-gown open to the navel will slump into the nearest chair and wait head in hands for mother to heat up the coffee, waving aside other nourishment. You will long since have learnt not to say a bright 'good morning'. The only response is silence; and the tactful thing to do is to slide across the papers, so that, after due pause, he can study the strip cartoons and the television programmes. Any discussion of the day's arrangements must be left for later, since at this point it will simply be met with: 'Christ, what do you expect me to say at this time in the morning?'

Outside the family circle, in bed-sitter land, the form is simply a perfunctory cup of instant coffee; and what vestiges remain of breakfast as a meal or a social occasion are likely to disappear with the threatened advent of television. With all conversation silenced by the commercials, the manufacturers of convenience foods will then have won their last battle for the breakfast table.

The question that remains is as to the nutritional value of a proper breakfast; and here one is on the shifting sands of popular dietetics, of

117

which the most widely-read manifestation is the pocket book on calorie counting. One has read books with stern warnings about carbohydrates, while others recommend a slimming diet of potatoes, and the manufacturers of breakfast cereals dwell on the residual protein content of their wares, often omitting to point out that it is, after all, the milk which is the body-building part of those bowls of crispy, golden, sugar-coated toasties. Others have suggested that one should *Eat Fat and Grow Slim*, or wax enthusiastic about tea (which has no nutritional value), recommending that one should avoid drinking it with milk (which has).

Without seeking to add to this proliferating and often contradictory advice, it seems worth stating a few basic physiological facts.

The average active male requires from 70-100 g a day of protein to repair loss of tissue from wear and tear, and additional energy, obtainable from a variety of foodstuffs, amounting to some 2500 calories. Women need some twenty per cent less food, and children considerably more protein for body-building purposes. In theory, it would be possible to obtain all this energy from proteins, but this would impose unwanted strain on the kidneys in eliminating unwanted residues — hence the usefulness of carbohydrate and fats. Fruit, though of course a most desirable adjunct, will not, unless eaten in bulk, supply sufficient energy.

The argument over what does and does not constitute an adequate breakfast hinges on the vexed question of the assimilation and maintenance of sufficient blood sugar to supply the body's need for energy during a morning's work. A cup of unsweetened black coffee supplies no energy at all, whilst even a large cup with sugar and milk is the equivalent of only 100 calories.

Calorie-counting is not a sufficient guide, since clinical studies in the U.S.A. have shown that after a breakfast high in carbohydrates — such as cereal, toast and marmalade — there is a rapid rise in blood sugar, falling off long before lunch owing to overproduction of insulin and withdrawal of sugar from the bloodstream. Proteins both stimulate the metabolism and, when eaten with carbohydrates and fat, result in a more gradual and much longer-lasting absorption of nutritives by the blood and tissues. The conclusion is that the traditional breakfast of bacon and eggs, toast and marmalade and milky coffee or tea, or a high protein breakfast of lean beef, cottage cheese and skim milk, produce outstanding results, ensuring 'a high level of efficiency'.

Dieticians, notwithstanding, continue to debate the issue, and a recent book argues that if a breakfast high in carbohydrate is good enough for millions of Continentals, it should serve for native Britons — who do not at the moment noticeably surpass them in energy or efficiency. This is perhaps to overlook the fact that the Spaniard, for example, supplements his *churros*, or bread and *confituras*, with a hearty mid-morning *bocadillo*, a crusty roll containing ham or sausage.

Perhaps the last word may be given to *Black's Medical Dictionary*:

> The *source* of food is not indifferent. It might be thought that a person well fed on peas would have the same powers as one fed on their equivalent in beef, but those races and individuals who feed upon a largely animal diet are characterised by the power of doing work more rapidly, by greater spirit, and by greater power of resisting disease.

It adds that, although this is undeniably true in general, 'it may be carried to a very fanciful extreme, as in the case of Kean, the actor, who would choose his dinner according to the part he was to play, taking pork for a tyrant, beef for a murderer, and mutton for a lover. Probably, in such a case, ease of digestion had more to do with the effect of food than its source.'

Most of us eat rather more than we should, without any marked ill effects, thanks to the compensating mechanisms of the body. Although many very fat people, from Henry VIII to Edward VII downwards, have been great eaters and gourmets — not to say gluttons — the most recent research goes to show that the fault is not entirely their own, but stems from a lazy metabolism; and this, it seems, is a result of a low level of 'brown fat', a substance found in localized areas of the body and instrumental in dissipating excessive nutriment.

The very aroma of freshly-made coffee or the sight of an appetizing plate of eggs, bacon, mushrooms or what you will, are an adjunct, since, as the knowledgeable *Black* points out, 'the gastric juice begins to be secreted even before the food enters the stomach, at the sight and smell of food (psychic secretion)'. And inveterate wine drinkers can take comfort from the fact that the pH (or acid) value of wine, unlike that of its more aqueous competitors, approximates to that of saliva. It therefore aids mastication and digestion in a way that 'water sole by itself' does not, as the percipient Dr Andrew Borde stressed so emphatically centuries ago.

We suspect that none of the above will alter individual breakfasting habits one iota. Clearly there were periods in the history of these Islands when the well-to-do indulged themselves far too freely at the breakfast-table — the bloated, gout-ridden figures caricatured by Gillray, Rowlandson and Leech are proof enough. On the other hand, the modern habit of fasting for most of the day and eating the heaviest meal increasingly late can only result in indigestion, restless nights and light sleep; and what does emerge is that the normal person, without weight problems and with a taste for a good, traditional British breakfast, can only benefit from it.

Index of Breakfast Foods

General Index

Page numbers in *italic* refer to the illustrations

124

150 YEARS' REPUTATION.

Keen's Mustard

As supplied to H.M. the QUEEN and H.R.H. the PRINCE OF WALES.

ROBINSON'S Pure Scotch OATMEAL.

Dr. PYE H. CHAVASSE: "Very pure, sweet, and good."

KEEN, ROBINSON, & CO., Ltd.,

MANUFACTURERS OF

ROBINSON'S PATENT GROATS.

ROBINSON'S PATENT BARLEY.

THE PERFECT WHEAT FOOD.

DAINTY. NOURISHING.

"FAROLA is immeasurably superior to arrowroot, cornflour, sago, &c. With milk it forms exquisite pudding,—and in the nursery it will prove a valuable variety which children will take with avidity."—*Liverpool Medico-Chirurgical Journal.*

"An ideal form of giving farinaceous food with milk."—*A London Physician.*

"Marlborough House, Pall Mall, S.W.—Colonel Clarke, Private Secretary to the Princess of Wales, writes to inform Mr. James Marshall that FAROLA has been ordered for use in the Household."

Awarded Gold Medals at the two important International Exhibitions held in 1886—Edinburgh and Liverpool—*two years before any imitations were in the market.*

FAROLA is a highly refined preparation of Wheat, which conserves all the nutritive elements and fine flavour naturally belonging to the purest part of the grain. All irritating and indigestible matter has been removed by careful treatment, mechanical means only being employed.

FAROLA will satisfy a robust appetite, but it is specially suited for invalids and children.

Send Post Card for Descriptive Book with Recipes (post free).

JAMES MARSHALL, 25, East Cumberland Street, GLASGOW.

BARTON & CO.,
Wine Merchants & Shippers,

CHIEF OFFICES: 59, ST. JAMES' STREET, LONDON, S.W.,
Where all Correspondence should be addressed.

CITY OFFICES AND CELLARS: 17, GRACECHURCH STREET, E.C.,
AND ST. MILDRED'S COURT, POULTRY, E.C.

Champagne.	Vintage 1878 and 1880.			
	70/- 72/- 74/- 78/- 84/- 96/- 100/- According to date of landing, quantity, and degree of excellence.			

Also a large Stock of 1874 choice brand.d Champagnes, from 100/- to 180/- per doz.

Claret.	Light Dinner.	Higher Class—First, Second, & Third Growths.					
		1878	1876	1879	1877	1872	1875
	12/- to 30/-	36/-	42/-	48/-	54/-	60/-	72/-

Also a large Stock of Latour, Leoville, Barton, and Lafite, 1864, 1871, 1875.

Sherry.	Pale, Pale Dry, Superior Pale.	Gold, Brown, Amber.	Manzanillas, Montillas, Vino de Pastos, Amontillados.	Old in Bottle of all the choicest varieties.
	21/- to 42/-	24/- to 54/-	32/- to 72/-	84/- to 140/- According to age and character.

Port.	Light or full-bodied.	Choice, Dry, Rich, & excellent flavour, from the wood and old in bottle.	Fine Natural.	VINTAGES.
				1820, 1834, 1840, 1847, 1851, 1853, 1854, 1863, 1870.
	20/- to 36/-	40/- to 60/-	48/- to 72/-	

Chablis, Sauterne, Madeira, Hock, Moselle, Marsala, Burgundy, Brandy, Whisky, and Liqueurs.

CUSTOMERS VISITING LONDON FOR SHORT PERIODS CAN HAVE THEIR CELLARS STOCKED ON SALE OR RETURN.

Decanted bottles of Claret, &c., for tasting, sent on receipt of telegram or letter.

BARTON & CO.'S HOUSE HAS BEEN ESTABLISHED OVER 100 YEARS.

CHOCOL

B

L

S

AWARDED

Annual C

26,0

SOLD RET

BELLAMY BROS.,

POULTERERS AND GAME-DEALERS,

118, JERMYN STREET, ST. JAMES'S.

THE LARGEST STOCK IN LONDON.

PRICES ON APPLICATION.

Country Orders Promptly Executed.

TELEPHONE No. 3735.

Possessing all the properties of the Finest Arrowroot,

BROWN & POLSON'S
CORN FLOUR

Is a World-Wide Necessary
FOR

THE NURSERY, THE SICK-ROOM, AND THE FAMILY TABLE.

NOTE.—Purchasers of Corn Flour should insist on being supplied with BROWN & POLSON'S. It is distinguished for uniformly superior quality.

BARTO

Wine, Spir

21, HAY

SPE

FINE

White Wine

CHUTNEES

HAM

Gorgona Anch

SEVILLE

EXTRAORDINARY TEA.

COOPER COOPER & CO.

ARE NOW SELLING

TEA

QUITE PHENOMENAL
IN QUALITY.

THE FINEST THE WORLD PRODUCES

At 3s. A POUND.
AND

MAGNIFICENT TEAS

At 2s. 6d. and 2s. a Pound,

As supplied to Princes, Dukes, Marquises, Earls, Viscounts, Barons, and the County Families of the United Kingdom.

Samples and Book about TEA post free on application to

COOPER COOPER & CO.

CHIEF OFFICE:
50, KING WILLIAM STREET, LONDON BRIDGE.

BRANCH ESTABLISHMENTS:

63, BISHOPSGATE ST. WITHIN, E.C.	268, REGENT CIRCUS, W.
38, STRAND (near Charing Cross), W.C.	7, WESTBOURNE GROVE, W.

334, HIGH HOLBORN, W.C.
LONDON.

ADAMS & SON,
MANUFACTURING AND FURNISHING IRONMONGERS,
Electro-Platers and Cutlers,
By Appointment to Her Majesty the Queen and H.R.H. the Prince of Wales.

57, HAYMARKET, S.W.

Stockpot.   Bainmarie.   Stewpan.

BEST HOUSE IN THE TRADE FOR

KITCHEN REQUISITES, MOULDS, and all the latest PARISIAN NOVELTIES and SPECIALITIES FOR THE CUISINE, *Special attention being given to this Department.*

DEPOT FOR CAPTAIN WARREN'S PATENT COOKING POTS.

10 PER CENT DISCOUNT ALLOWED FOR CASH.
Illustrated Catalogue forwarded on application.

57, HAYMARKET, S.W.

GRAND MEDAL

JAMES

DU

MAR

ONLY PRIZE ME

LON

ENIER

t

MENIER
MENIER
MENIER
MENIER
MENIER
MENIER

n

E MEDALS.

n exceeds

lbs.

RYWHERE.

CHAMBERS, MONNERY, & CO.,
IRONMONGERS,
41, Bishopsgate St. Without, London (5 minutes from Bank of England).
THE "BISHOPSGATE" COOKING RANGE

This, the most popular Cooking Stove of the day, is used extensively throughout the Kingdom in small households, and in others **as an auxiliary to the larger Range**, and is, in every case, a complete and signal success.

FOUR "PRIZE MEDALS AWARDED.

TWO AT HEALTH EXHIBITION, 1884.

Ranges in Stock from 35s. to £16.

LOVELOCK'S
IMPROVED
MINCING & SAUSAGE MAKING MACHINES & COFFEE MILLS FOR DOMESTIC USE.

PRICES OF MINCERS.	PRICES OF COFFEE MILLS.
No. 1. 10s. 6d.	No. 1. 6s. 0d.
No. 2. 15s. 0d.	No. 2. 8s. 0d.
No. 3. 21s. 0d.	No. 3. 10s. 0d.
No. 4. 42s. 0d.	No. 4. 14s. 0d.

They are unrivalled for simplicity and efficiency, and for promoting domestic economy are invaluable in every household. Can be obtained of Ironmongers and Dealers in all parts of the World. Wholesale of
J. F. LOVELOCK, Broadway Works, Hamburg Street, Hackney, London.
ESTABLISHED 1856.

EMILE BEGUINOT,
MANUFACTURER OF
PRESERVED PROVISIONS,
GAME PÂTÉS, PÂTÉS DE GIBIER,
SOUPS IN CLASS BOTTLES.
Awarded Silver Medal, Cookery Exhibition, for Purity and Excellence

RAISED GAME PIES.
INVALIDS' SPECIALITIES:
Beef Tea, Chicken Broth, Turtle Jelly.

E. BEGUINOT'S
CELEBRATED ENTRÉE SAUCES,
Espagnole, Tomato, and Italian,
From 1s. per Bottle upwards.

ALL THE ABOVE ARTICLES CAN BE OBTAINED FROM ALL FIRST CLASS ITALIAN WAREHOUSEMEN.

N.B.—Upwards of 12 years Chef de Cuisine to Earl Granville.

2, ST. JAMES' STREET, S.W.,
8, RUE DE MOSCOU, PARIS,
AND
401½, WANDSWORTH ROAD, LONDON, S.W.

Procter & Company,
DIRECT IMPORTERS OF

Udiapore • Shields.
Punjaub Shields.
Rajpootana • Swords.
Nepaulese Swords.
Lahore • Daggers.
Peshawar Daggers.
Kattiawar • Maces.
Kattiawar • Axes.

The Indian Art Gallery, 428, Oxford St., near Orchard Street.

DASH & Co.,
FISHMONGERS,
OYSTER AND ICE MERCHANTS,
99, JERMYN STREET, ST. JAMES'S,
LONDON.

BEST CLASS ONLY.
BILL OF FARE ON APPLICATION.
COUNTRY ORDERS PUNCTUALLY ATTENDED TO.
TELEPHONE No. 3736.

E & Co.,

r Merchants,
ET, S.W.

TIES.

ALADS.

and Flavoured.

, PICKLES,
GUES,
in Brine & Oil.
ARMALADE.

FLORADOR

8 Gold MEDALS

THE GREAT WHEAT FOOD

FLORADOR is made in three sizes of grains.

Large Grained for Porridge, Omelettes, Soups, &c.
Medium Grained for Baked or Boiled Puddings, &c.
Fine Grained for Blanc Mange, Cakes, Creams, Infants' Foods, &c.

RECIPES ON PACKETS

The *Lancet* says :—" This preparation is excellent."

To be had at Stores and Grocers in ½ and 1 lb.
Packets at 6d. per lb., or from Chemists in
2/- Tins.

FLORADOR FOOD CO.,
90, Washington St., Glasgow.
LONDON DEPOT: COWAN & Co., 28 & 29, LONDON WALL, E.C.

VIENNA 1873

& SON'S
E
DE
MARMALADE
62

SILVER MEDAL, HEALTH EXHIBITION, 1884.
SUGG'S NEW PATENT
"CHARING CROSS" GAS KITCHENER.
Roasts, Boils, Fries, Grills, and Bakes Pastry and Bread.

The Meat is really roasted in fresh air as before a cool fire, and the flavour preserved better than by any other method.

May be seen in action and tested every day at our Show Rooms,
1 & 2, GRAND HOTEL BUILDINGS, CHARING CROSS.
WILLIAM SUGG & Co.,
LIMITED.